Narrative of Henry Box Brown

Who escaped slavery enclosed in a box 3 feet long and 2 wide

Henry Box Brown

TABLE OF CONTENTS

Preface

Narrative

Cure for the Evil of Slavery (by Charles Stearns)

Footnotes

PREFACE

NOT for the purpose of administering to a prurient desire to "hear and see some new thing," nor to gratify any inclination on the part of the hero of the following story to be honored by man, is this simple and touching narrative of the perils of a seeker after the "boon of liberty," introduced to the public eye; but that the people of this country may be made acquainted with the horrid sufferings endured by one as, in a portable prison, shut out from the light of heaven, and nearly deprived of its balmy air, he pursued his fearful journey directly through the heart of a country making its boasts of liberty and freedom to all, and that thereby a chord of human sympathy may be touched in the hearts of those who listen to his plaintive tale, which may be the means of furthering the spread of those principles, which under God, shall yet prove "mighty to the pulling down of the strong-holds" of slavery.

O reader, as you peruse this heart-rending tale, let the tear of sympathy roll freely from your eyes, and let the deep fountains of human feeling, which God has implanted in the breast of every son and daughter of Adam, burst forth from their enclosure, until a stream shall flow therefrom on to the surrounding world, of so invigorating and purifying a nature, as to arouse from the "death of the sin" of slavery, and cleanse from the pollutions thereof, all with whom you may be connected. As Henry Box Brown's thrilling escape is portrayed before you, let it not be perused by you as an idle tale, while you go away "forgetting what manner of persons you are;" but let truth find an avenue through your sensibilities, by which it can reach the citadel of your soul, and there dwell in all its life-giving power, expelling the whole brotherhood of pro-slavery errors, which politicians, priests, and selfish avarice, have introduced to the acquaintance of your intellectual faculties. These faculties are oftener blinded by selfishness, than are imbecile of themselves, as the powerful intellect of a Webster is led captive to the inclinations of a not unselfish heart; so that that which should be the ruling power of every man's nature, is held in degrading submission to the inferior feelings of his heart. If man is blinded to the appreciation of the good, by a mass of selfish sensibilities, may he not be induced to surrender his will to the influence of truth, by benevolent feelings being caused to spring forth in his heart? That this may be the case with all whose eyes gaze upon the picture here drawn of misery, and of endurance, worthy of a Spartan, and such as a hero of olden times might be proud of, and transmit to posterity, along with the armorial emblazonry of his ancestors, is the ardent desire of all connected with the publication of this work. A word in regard to the literary character of the tale before you. The narrator is freshly from a land where books and schools are forbidden under severe penalties, to all in his former condition, and of course knoweth not letters, having never learned them; but of his capabilities otherwise, no one can doubt, when they recollect that if the records of all nations, from the time when Adam and Eve first placed their free feet upon the soil of Eden, until the conclusion of the scenes depicted by Hildreth and Macaulay, should be diligently searched, a parallel instance of heroism, in behalf of personal liberty, could not be found. Instances of fortitude for the defence of religious freedom, and in cases of a violation of conscience being required; and for the sake of offspring, of friends and of one's country are not uncommon; but whose heroism and ability to contrive, united, have equalled our friend's whose story is now before you?[1]

A William and an Ellen Craft, indeed performed an almost equally hazardous undertaking, and one which, as a devoted admirer of human daring has said, far exceeded any thing recorded by Macaulay, and will yet be made the ground-work for a future Scott to build a more intensely interesting tale upon than "the author of Waverly" ever put forth, but they had the benefit of their eyes and ears—they were not entirely helpless; enclosed in a moving tomb, and as utterly destitute of power to control your movements as if death had fastened its icy arm upon you, and yet possessing all the full tide of gushing sensibilities, and a complete knowledge of your existence, as was the case with our friend. We read with horror of the burial of persons before life has entirely fled from them, but here is a man who voluntarily assumed a condition in which he well knew all the chances were against him, and when his head seemed well-nigh severed from his body, on account of the concussion occasioned by the rough handling to which he was subject, see the Spartan firmness of his soul. Not a groan escaped from his agonized heart, as the realities of his condition were so vividly presented before him. Death stared him in the face, but like Patrick Henry, only when the alternative was more a matter of fact than it was to that patriot, he exclaims, "Give me liberty or give me death;" and death seemed to say, as quickly as the lion seizes the kid cast into its den, "You are already mine," and was about to wrap its sable mantle around the form of our self-martyred hero—bound fast upon the altars of freedom, as the Hindoo widow is bound upon the altar of a husband's love; when the bright angel of liberty, whose dazzling form he had so long and so anxiously watched, as he pored over the scheme hid in the recesses of his own fearless brain, while yet a slave, and whose shining eyes had bewitched his soul, until he had said in the language of one of old to Jesus, "I will follow thee whithersoever thou goest;" when this blessed goddess stood at his side, and, as Jesus said to one lying cold in death's embrace, "I say unto thee, arise," said to him, as she took him by the hand and lifted him from his travelling tomb, "thy warfare is over, thy work is accomplished, a free man art thou, my guidance has availed thee, arise and breathe the air of freedom."

Did Lazarus astonish his weeping sisters, and the surrounding multitude, as he emerged from his house of clay, clad in the habiliments of the grave, and did joy unfeigned spread throughout that gazing throng? How much more astonishing seemed the birth of

Mr. Brown, as he "came forth" from a box, clothed not in the habiliments of the grave, but in those of slavery, worse than the "silent house of death," as his acts had testified; and what greater joy thrilled through the wondering witnesses, as the lid was removed from the travelling carriage of our friend's electing, and straightway arose therefrom a living man, a being made in God's own image, a son of Jehovah, whom the piety and republicanism of this nation had doomed to pass through this terrible ordeal, before the wand of the goddess of liberty could complete his transformation from a slave to a free man! But we will desist from further comments. Here is the plain narrative of our friend, and is it asking too much of you, whose sympathies may be aroused by the recital which follows, to continue to peruse these pages until the cause of all his sufferings is depicted before you, and your duty under the circumstances is clearly pointed out?

Here are the identical words uttered by him as soon as he inhaled the fresh air of freedom, after the faintness occasioned by his sojourn in his temporary tomb had passed away.

HYMN OF THANKSGIVING, SUNG BY HENRY BOX BROWN, After being released from his confinement in the Box, at Philadelphia.

I waited patiently, I waited patiently for the Lord, for the Lord,

And he inclined unto me, and heard my calling;

I waited patiently, I waited patiently for the Lord,

And he inclined unto me, and heard my calling;

And he hath put a new song in my mouth,

Ev'n a thanksgiving, Ev'n a thanksgiving, Ev'n a thanksgiving unto our God.

Blessed, Blessed, Blessed, Blessed is the man, Blessed is the man,

Blessed is the man that hath set his hope, his hope in the Lord;

O Lord my God, Great, Great, Great,

Great are the wondrous works which thou hast done,

Great are the wondrous works which thou hast done, which thou hast done,

Great are the wondrous works,

Great are the wondrous works,

Great are the wondrous works, which thou hast done.

If I should declare them and speak of them, they should be more,

more, more than I am able to express.

I have not kept back thy loving kindness and truth from the great congregation,

I have not kept back thy loving kindness and truth from the great congregation.

Withdraw not thou thy mercy from me,

Withdraw not thou thy mercy from me, O Lord;

Let thy loving kindness and thy truth always preserve me,

Let all those that seek thee be joyful and glad,

Let all those that seek thee, be joyful and glad, be joyful, be glad, be joyful and glad, be joyful, be joyful, be joyful, be joyful, be joyful and glad, be glad in thee.

And let such as love thy salvation,

And let such as love thy salvation, say always,

The Lord be praised,

The Lord be praised:

Let all those that seek thee be joyful and glad,

And let such as love thy salvation, say always,

The Lord be praised,

The Lord be praised,

The Lord be praised.

Boston, Sept. 1, 1849.

NARRATIVE

I AM not about to harrow the feelings of my readers by a terrific representation of the untold horrors of that fearful system of oppression, which for thirty-three long years entwined its snaky folds about my soul, as the serpent of South America coils itself around the form of its unfortunate victim. It is not my purpose to descend deeply into the dark and noisome caverns of the hell of slavery, and drag from their frightful abode those lost spirits who haunt the souls of the poor slaves, daily and nightly with their frightful presence, and with the fearful sound of their terrific instruments of torture; for other pens far abler than mine have effectually performed that portion of the labor of an exposer of the enormities of slavery. Slavery, like the shield discovered by the knights of olden time, has two diverse sides to it; the one, on which is fearfully written in letters of blood, the character of the mass who carry on that dreadful system of unhallowed bondage; the other, touched with the pencil of a gentler delineator, and telling the looker on, a tale of comparative freedom, from the terrible deprivations so vividly portrayed on its opposite side.

My book will present, if possible, the beautiful side of the picture of slavery; will entertain you with stories of partial kindness on the part of my master, and of comparative enjoyment on my own part, as I grew up under the benign influence of the blessed system so closely connected with our "republican institutions," as Southern politicians tell us.

From the time I first breathed the air of human existence, until the hour of my escape from bondage, I did not receive but one whipping. I never suffered from lack of food, or on account of too extreme labor; nor for want of sufficient clothing to cover my person. My tale is not, therefore, one of horrid inflictions of the lash upon my naked body; of cruel starvings and of insolent treatment; but is the very best representation of slavery which can be given; therefore, reader, allow me to inform you, as you, for aught I know, may be one of those degraded mortals who fancy that if no blows are inflicted upon the slave's body, and a plenty of "bread and bacon" is dealed out to him, he is therefore no sufferer, and slavery is not a cruel institution; allow me to inform you, that I did not escape from such deprivations. It was not for fear of the lash's dreaded infliction, that I endured that fearful imprisonment, which you are waiting to read concerning; nor because of destitution of the necessaries of life, did I enclose myself in my travelling prison, and traverse your boasted land of freedom, a portion of the time with my head in an inverted position, as if it were a terrible crime for me to endeavor to escape from slavery.

Far beyond, in terrible suffering, all outward cruelties of the foul system, are those inner pangs which rend the heart of fond affection, when the "bone of your bone, and the flesh of your flesh" is separated from your embrace, by the ruthless hand of the merciless tyrant, as he plucks from your heart of love, the one whom God hath given you for a "help-meet" through the journey of life; and more fearful by far than all the blows of the bloody lash, or the pangs of cruel hunger are those lashings of the heart, which the best of slaveholders inflict upon their happy and "well off" slaves, as they tear from their grasp the pledges of love, smiling at the side of devoted attachment. Tell me not of kind masters under slavery's hateful rule! There is no such thing as a person of that description; for, as you will see, my master, one of the most distinguished of this uncommon class of slaveholders, hesitated not to allow the wife of my love to be torn from my fond embrace, and the darling idols of my heart, my little children, to be snatched from my arms, and thus to doom them to a separation from me, more dreadful to all of us than a large number of lashes, inflicted on us daily. And yet to this fate I was continually subject, during a large portion of the time, when heaven seemed to smile propitiously above me; and no black clouds of fearful character lowered over my head. Heaven save me from kind masters, as well as from those called more cruel; for even their "tender mercies are cruel," and what no freeman could endure for a moment. My tale necessarily lacks that thrilling interest which is attached to the more than romantic, although perfectly true descriptions of a life in slavery, given by my numerous forerunners in the work of sketching a slave's personal experience; but I shall endeavor to intermingle with it other scenes which came under my own observation, which will serve to convince you, that if I was spared a worse fate than actually fell to my lot, yet my comrades around me were not so fortunate; but were the victims of the ungovernable rage of those men, of whose characters one cannot be informed, without experiencing within his soul, a rushing of overflowing emotions of pity, indignation and horror.

I first drew the breath of life in Louisa County, Va., forty-five miles from the city of Richmond, in the year 1816. I was born a slave. Not because at the moment of my birth an angel stood by, and declared that such was the will of God concerning me; although in a country whose most honored writings declare that all men have a right to liberty, given them by their Creator, it seems strange that I, or any of my brethren, could have been born without this inalienable right, unless God had thus signified his departure from his usual rule, as described by our fathers. Not, I say, on account of God's willing it to be so, was I born a slave, but for the reason that nearly all the people of this country are united in legislating against heaven, and have contrived to vote down our heavenly father's rules, and to substitute for them, that cruel law which binds the chains of slavery upon one sixth part of the inhabitants of this land. I was born a slave! and wherefore? Tyrants, remorseless, destitute of religion and principle, stood by the couch of my mother, as heaven placed a pure soul, in the infantile form, there lying in her arms—a new being, never having breathed earth's atmosphere before; and fearlessly, with no compunctions of remorse, stretched forth their bloody arms and pressed the life of God from me, baptizing my soul and body as their own property; goods and chattels in their hands! Yes, they robbed me of myself, before I could know the nature of their wicked acts; and for ever afterwards, until I took possession of my own soul and body, did they retain their stolen property. This was why I was born a slave. Reader, can you understand the horrors of that fearful name? Listen, and I will assist you in this difficult work. My father, and my mother of course, were slaves before me; but both of them are now enjoying the invaluable boon of liberty, having purchased themselves, in this land of freedom! At an early age, my mother would take me on her knee, and pointing to the forest trees adjacent, now being stripped of their thick foliage by autumnal winds, would say to me, "my son, as yonder leaves are stripped from off the trees of the forest, so are the children of slaves swept away from them by the hands of cruel tyrants;" and her voice would tremble, and she would seem almost choked with her deep emotions, while the big tears would find their way down her saddened cheeks, as she fondly pressed me to her heaving bosom, as if to save me from so dreaded a calamity. I was young then, but I well recollect the sadness of her countenance, and the mournfulness of her words, and they made a deep impression upon my youthful mind. Mothers of the North, as you gaze upon the free forms of your idolized little ones, as they playfully and confidently move around you, O if you knew that the lapse of a few years would infallibly remove them from your affectionate care, not to be laid in the silent grave, "where the wicked cease from troubling," but to be the sport of cruel men, and the victims of barbarous tyrants, who would snatch them from your side, as the robber seizes upon the bag of gold in the traveller's hand; O, would not your life then be rendered a miserable one indeed? Who can trace the workings of a slave mother's soul, as she counts over the hours, the departure of which, she almost knows, will rob her of her darling children, and consign them to a fate more horrible than death's cold embrace! O, who can hear of these cruel deprivations, and not be aroused to action in the slave's behalf?

My mother used to instruct me in the principles of morality, as much as she was able; but I was deplorably ignorant on religious subjects, for what ideas can a slave have of religion, when those who profess it around him, are demons in human shape oftentimes, as you will presently see was the case with my master's overseer? My mother used to tell me not to steal, and not to lie, and to behave myself properly in other respects. She took a great deal of pains with me and my brother; which resulted in our endeavors to conduct ourselves with propriety. As a specimen of the religious knowledge of the slaves, I will state here my ideas in regard to my master; assuring the reader that I am not joking, but stating what was the opinion of all the slave children on my master's plantation; and I have often talked it over with my early associates, and my mother, and enjoyed hearty laughs at the absurdity of our youthful ideas.

I really believed my old master was Almighty God, and that his son, my young master, was Jesus Christ.[2]

One reason I had for this belief was, that when it was about to thunder, my old master would approach us, if we were in the yard, and say, "All you children run into the house now, for it is going to thunder," and after the shower was over, we would go out again, and he would approach us smilingly, and say, "What a fine shower we have had," and bidding us look at the flowers in the garden, would say, "how pretty the flowers look now." We thought that he thundered, and caused the rain to fall; and not until I was eight years of age, did I get rid of this childish superstition. Our master was uncommonly kind, and as he moved about in his dignity, he seemed like a god to us, and probably he did not dislike our reverential feelings towards him. All the slaves called his son, our Saviour, and the way I was enlightened on this point was as follows. One day after returning from church, my mother told father of a woman who wished to join the church. She told the preacher she had been baptized by one of the slaves, who was called from his office, "John the Baptist;" and on being asked by the minister if she believed "that our Saviour came into the world, and had died for the sins of man," she replied, that she "knew he had come into the world," but she "had not heard he was dead, as she lived so far from the road, she did not learn much that was going on in the world." I then asked mother, if young master was dead. She said it was not him they were talking about; it was "our Saviour in heaven." I then asked her if there were two Saviours, when she told me that young master was not "our Saviour," which filled me with astonishment, and I could not understand it at first. Not long after this, my sister became anxious to have her soul converted, and shaved the hair from her head, as many of the slaves thought they could not be converted without doing this. My mother reproved her, and began to tell her of God who dwelt in heaven, and that she must pray to him to convert her. This surprised me still more, and I asked her if old master was not God; to which she replied that he was not, and began to instruct me a little in reference to the God of heaven. After this, I believed there was a God who ruled the world, but I did not previously, have the least idea of any such being. And why should not my childish fancy be correct, according to the blasphemous teachings of the heathen system of slavery? Does not every slaveholder assume exclusive control over all the actions of his unfortunate victims? Most assuredly he does, as this extract from the laws of a slaveholding State will show you. "A slave is one who is in the power of his master, to whom he belongs. A slave owes to his master and all his family, respect without bounds and absolute obedience." How tallies this with the unalterable law of Jehovah, "Thou shalt have no other gods before me?" Does not the system of slavery effectually shut out from the slave's heart, all true knowledge of the eternal God, and doom him to grope his perilous way, amid the thick darkness of unenlightened heathenism, although he dwells in a land professing much religion, and an entire freedom from the superstitions of paganism?

Let me tell you my opinion of the slaveholding religion of this land. I believe in a hell, where the wicked will forever dwell, and knowing the character of slaveholders and slavery, it is my settled belief, as it was while I was a slave, even though I was treated kindly, that every slaveholder will infallibly go to that hell, unless he repents. I do not believe in the religion of the Southern churches, nor do I perceive any great difference between them, and those at the North, which uphold them.

While a young lad, my principal employment was waiting upon my master and mistress, and at intervals taking lessons in what is the destiny of most of the slaves, the cultivation of the plantation. O how often as the hot sun sent forth its scorching rays upon my tender head, did I look forward with dismay, to the time, when I, like my fellow slaves, should be driven by the task-master's cruel lash, to the performance of unrequited toil upon the plantation of my master. To this expectation is the slave trained. Like the criminal under sentence of death, he notches upon his wooden stick, as Sterne's captive did, the days, after the lapse of which he must be introduced to his dreaded fate; in the case of the criminal, merely death—a cessation from the pains and toils of life; but in our cases, the commencement of a living death; a death never ending, second in horror only to the eternal torment of the wicked in a future state. Yea, even worse than that, for there, a God of love and mercy holds the rod of punishment in his own hand; but in our case, it is held by men from whom almost the last vestige of goodness has departed, and in whose hearts there dwells hardly a spark of humanity, certainly not enough to keep them from the practice of the most inhuman crimes. Imagine, reader, a fearful cloud, gathering blackness as it advances towards you, and increasing in size constantly; hovering in the deep blue vault of the firmament above you, which cloud seems loaded with the elements of destruction, and from the contents of which you are certain you cannot escape. You are sailing upon the now calm waters of the broad and placid deep, spreading its "unadorned bosom" before you, as far as your eye can reach, "Calm as a slumbering babe, Tremendous Ocean lays;" and on its "burnished waves," gracefully rides your little vessel, without fear or dismay troubling your heart. But this fearful cloud is pointed out to you, and as it gathers darkness, and rushes to the point of the firmament overhanging your fated vessel, O what terror then seizes upon your soul, as hourly you expect your little bark to be deluged by the contents of the cloud, and riven by the fierce lightnings enclosed in that mass of angry elements. So with the slave, only that he knows his chances of escape are exceedingly small, while you may very likely outlive the storm.

To this terrible apprehension we are all constantly subject. To-day, master may smile lovingly upon us, and the sound of the cracking whip may be hushed, but the dread uncertainty of our future fate still hangs over us, and to-morrow may witness a return of all the elements of fearful strife, as we emphatically "know not what a day may bring forth." The sweet songsters of the air, as it were, may warble their musical notes ever so melodiously, harmonizing with the soft-blowing of the western winds which invigorates our frames, and the genial warmth of the early sun may fill us with pleasurable emotions; but we know that ere long, this sweet singing must be silenced by the fierce cracking of the bloody lash, falling on our own shoulders, and that the cool breezes and the gentle heat of early morn, must be succeeded by the hot winds and fiery rays of Slavery's meridian day. The slave has no certainty of the enjoyment of any privilege whatever! All his fancied blessings, without a moment's warning being granted to him, may be swept forever from his trembling grasp. Who will then say that "disguise itself" as Slavery will, it is not "a bitter cup," the mixture whereof is gall and wormwood?

My brother and myself, were in the practice of carrying grain to mill, a few times a year, which was the means of furnishing us with some information respecting other slaves. We often went twenty miles, to a mill owned by a Col. Ambler, in Yansinville county, and used to improve our opportunities for gaining information. Especially desirous were we, of learning the condition of slaves around us, for we knew not how long we should remain in as favorable hands as we were then. On one occasion, while waiting for our grain, we entered a house in the neighborhood, and while resting ourselves there, we saw a number of forlorn-looking beings pass the door, and as they passed, we noticed that they turned and gazed earnestly upon us. Afterwards, about fifty performed the same act, which excited our minds somewhat, as we overheard some of them say, "Look there, and see those two colored men with shoes, vests and hats on," and we determined to obtain an interview with them. Accordingly, after receiving some bread and meat from our hosts, we followed these abject beings to their quarters;—and such a sight we had never witnessed before, as we had always lived on our master's plantation, and this was about the first of our journeys to the mill. They were dressed with shirts made of coarse bagging, such as coffee-sacks are made from, and some kind of light substance for pantaloons, and no other clothing whatever. They had on no shoes, hats, vests, or coats, and when my brother asked them why they spoke of our being dressed with those articles of clothing, they said they had "never seen negroes dressed in that way before." They looked very hungry, and we divided our bread and meat among them, which furnished them only a mouthful each. They never had any meat, they said, given them by their masters. My brother put various questions to them, such as, "if they had wives?" "did they go to church?" "had they any sisters?" &c. The one who gave us the information, said they had wives, but were obliged to marry on their own plantation. Master would not allow them to go away from home to marry, consequently he said they were all related to each other, and master made them marry, whether related or not. My brother asked this man to show him his sisters; he said he could not tell them from the rest, they were all his sisters; and here let me state, what is well known by many people, that no such thing as real marriage is allowed to exist among the slaves. Talk of marriage under such a system! Why, the owner of a Turkish harem, or the keeper of a house of ill-fame, might as well allow the inmates of their establishments to marry as for a Southern slaveholder to do the same. Marriage, as is well known, is the voluntary and perfect union of one man with one woman, without depending upon the will of a third party. This never can take place under slavery, for the moment a slave is allowed to form such a connection as he chooses, the spell of slavery is dissolved. The slave's wife is his, only at the will of her master, who may violate her chastity with impunity. It is my candid opinion that one of the strongest motives which operate upon the slaveholders, and induce them to retain their iron grasp upon the unfortunate slave, is because it gives them such unlimited control in this respect over the female slaves. The greater part of slaveholders are licentious men, and the most respectable and the kindest of masters, keep some of their slaves as mistresses. It is for their pecuniary interest to do so in several respects. Their progeny is so many dollars and cents in their pockets, instead of being a bill of expense to them, as would be the case if their slaves were free; and mulatto slaves command a higher price than dark colored ones; but it is too horrid a subject to describe. Suffice it to say, that no slave has the least certainty of being able to retain his wife or her husband a single hour; so that the slave is placed under strong inducements not to form a union of love, for he knows not how soon the chords wound around his heart would be snapped asunder, by the hand of the brutal slave-dealer. Northern people sustain slavery, knowing that it is a system of perfect licentiousness, and yet go to church and boast of their purity and holiness!

On this plantation, the slaves were never allowed to attend church, but managed their religious affairs in their own way. An old slave, whom they called Uncle John, decided upon their piety, and would baptize them during the silent watches of the night, while their master was "taking his rest in sleep." Thus is the slave under the necessity of even "saving his soul" in the hours when the eye of his master, who usurps the place of God over him, is turned from him. Think of it, ye who contend for the necessity of these rites, to constitute a man a Christian! By night must the poor slave steal away from his bed of straw, and leaving his miserable hovel, must drag his weary limbs to some adjacent stream of water, where a fellow slave, as ignorant as himself, proceeds to administer the ordinance of baptism; and as he plunges his comrades into the water, in imitation of the Baptist of old, how he trembles, lest the footsteps of his master should be heard, advancing to their Bethesda,—knowing that if such should be the case, the severe punishment that awaits them all. Baptists, are ye striking hands with Southern churches, which thus exclude so many slaves from the "waters of salvation?"

But we were obliged to cut short our conversation with these slaves, by beholding the approach of the overseer, who was directing his steps towards us, like a bear seeking its prey. We had only time to ask this man, "if they were often whipped?" to which he replied, "that not a day passed over their heads, without some of their number being brutally punished; and," said he, "we shall have to suffer for this talk with you." He then told us, that many of them had been severely whipped that very morning, for having been baptized the night before. After we left them, we looked back, and heard the screams of these poor creatures, suffering under the blows of the hard-hearted overseer, for the crime of talking with us;—which screams sounded in our ears for some time. We felt thankful that we were exempted from such terrible treatment; but still, we knew not how soon we should be subject to the same cruel fate. By this time we had returned to the mill, where we met a young man, (a relation of the owner of this plantation,) who for some time appeared to be eyeing us quite attentively. At length he asked me if I had "ever been whipped," and when I told him I had not, he replied, "Well, you will neither of you ever be of any value, then;" so true is it that whipping is considered a necessary part of slavery. Without this practice, it could not stand a single day. He expressed a good deal of surprise that we were allowed to wear hats and shoes,—supposing that a slave had no business to wear such clothing as his master wore. We had brought our fishing-lines with us, and requested the privilege to fish in his stream, which he roughly denied us, saying, "we do not allow niggers to fish." Nothing daunted, however, by this rebuff, my brother went to another place, and was quite successful in his undertaking, obtaining a plentiful supply of the finny tribe; but as soon as this youngster perceived his good luck, he ordered him to throw them back into the stream, which he was obliged to do, and we returned home without them.

We finally abandoned visiting this mill, and carried our grain to another, a Mr. Bullock's, only ten miles distant from our plantation. This man was very kind to us, took us into his house and put us to bed, took charge of our horses, and carried the grain himself into the mill, and in the morning furnished us with a good breakfast. I asked my brother why this man treated us so differently from our old miller. "Oh," said he, "this man is not a slaveholder!" Ah, that explained the difference; for there is nothing in the southern character averse to gentleness. On the contrary, if it were not for slavery's withering touch, the Southerners would be the kindest people in the land. Slavery possesses the power attributed to one of old, of changing the nature of all who drink of its vicious cup.

"——— ——— ——— *Which, as they taste,*

Soon as the potion works, their human countenance,

The express resemblance of the gods, is changed

Into some brutish form of wolf, or bear,

Or ounce, or tiger, hog, or bearded goat;

And they, so perfect is their misery,

Not once perceive their foul disfigurement,

But boast themselves more comely than before."

Under the influence of slavery's polluting power, the most gentle women become the fiercest viragos, and the most benevolent men are changed into inhuman monsters. It is true of the northern man who goes South also.

"Whoever tastes, loses his upright shape,

And downward falls, into a grovelling swine."

This non-slaveholder also allowed us to catch as many fish as we pleased, and even furnished us with fishing implements. While at this mill, we became acquainted with a colored man from another part of the country; and as our desire was strong to learn how our brethren fared in other places, we questioned him respecting his treatment. He complained much of his hard fate,—said he had a wife and one child, and begged for some of our fish to carry to his wife; which my brother gladly gave him. He said he was expecting to have some money in a few days, which would be "the first he ever had in his life!" He had sent a thousand hickory-nuts to market, for which he afterwards informed us he had received thirty-six cents, which he gave to his wife, to furnish her with some little article of comfort. This was the sum total of all the money he had ever been the possessor of! Ye northern pro-slavery men, do you regard this as robbery, or not? The whole of this man's earnings had been robbed from him during his entire life, except simply his coarse food and miserable clothing, the whole expense of which, for a plantation slave, does not exceed twenty dollars a year. This is one reason why I think every slaveholder will go to hell; for my Bible teaches me that no thief shall enter heaven; and I know every slaveholder is a thief; and I rather think you would all be of my opinion if you had ever been a slave. But now, assisting these thieves, and being made rich by them, you say they are not robbers; just as wicked men generally shield their abettors.

On our return from this place, we met a colored man and woman, who were very cross to each other. We inquired as to the cause of their trouble, and the man told us, that "women had such tongues!" that some of them had stolen a sheep, and this woman, after eating of it, went and told their master, and they all had to receive a severe whipping. And here follows a specimen of slaveholding morality, which will show you how much many of the masters care for their slaves' stealing. This man enjoined upon his slaves never to steal from him again, but to steal from his neighbors, and he would keep them from punishment, if they would furnish him with a portion of the meat! And why not? For is it any worse for the slaveholders to steal from one another, than it is to steal from their helpless slaves? Not long after, these slaves availed themselves of their master's assistance, and stole an animal from a neighboring plantation, and according to agreement, furnished their master with his share. Soon the owner of the missing animal came rushing into the man's house, who had just eaten of the stolen food, and, in a very excited manner, demanded reparation from him, for the beast stolen, as he said, by this man's slaves. The villain, hardly able to stand after eating so bountifully of his neighbor's pork, exclaimed loudly, "my servants know no more about your hogs than I do!" which was strictly true; and the loser of the swine went away satisfied. This man told his slaves that it was a sin to steal from him, but none to steal from his neighbors! My brother told the slave we were conversing with, that it was as much of a sin in God's sight, for him to steal from one, as from the other. "Oh," said the slave, "master says negroes have nothing to do with God!" He further informed us that his master and mistress lived very unhappily together, on account of the maid who waited upon them. She had no husband, but had several yellow children. After we left them, they went to a fodder-stack, and took out a jug, and drank of its contents. My brother's curiosity was excited to learn the nature of their drink; and watching his opportunity, unobserved by them, he slipped up to the stack, and ascertained that the jug was nearly full of Irish whiskey. He carried it home with him, and the next time we visited the mill, he returned the jug to its former place, filled with molasses, purchased with his own money, instead of the fiery drink which it formerly contained. Some time after this, the master of this man discovered a great falling off in the supply of stolen meat furnished him by the slaves, and questioned this man in reference to the cause of such a lamentable diminution in the supply of hog-meat in particular. The slave told him the story of the jug, and that he had ceased drinking, which was sad news for the pork-loving gentleman.

I will now return to my master's affairs. My young master's brother was a very benevolent man, and soon became convinced that it was wrong to hold men in bondage; which belief he carried into practice by emancipating forty slaves at one time, and paying the expenses of their transportation to a free state. But old master, although naturally more kind-hearted than his neighbors, could not always remain as impervious to the assaults of the pro-slavery demon; and as stated previously, that all who drank of this hateful cup were transformed into some vile animal, so he became a perfect brute in his treatment of his slaves. I cannot account for this change, only on the supposition, that experience had convinced him that kind treatment was not as well adapted to the production of crops, as a severer kind of discipline. Under the elating influence of freedom's inspiring sound, men will labor much harder, than when forced to perform unpleasant tasks, the accomplishment of which will be of no value to themselves; but while the slave is held as such, it is difficult for him to feel as he would feel, if he was a free man, however light may be his tasks, and however kind may be his master. The lash is still held above his head, and may fall upon him, even if its blows are for a long time withheld. This the slave realizes; and hence no kind treatment can destroy the depressing influence of a consciousness of his being a slave,—no matter how lightly the yoke of slavery may rest upon his shoulders. He knows the yoke is there; and that at any time its weight may be made heavier, and his form almost sink under its weary burden; but give him his liberty, and new life enters into him immediately. The iron yoke falls from his chafed shoulders; the collar, even if it was a silken one, is removed from his enslaved person; and the chains, although made of gold, fall from his bound limbs, and he walks forth with an elastic step, to enjoy the realities of his new existence. Now he is ready to perform irksome tasks; for the avails of his labor will be of value to himself, and with them he can administer comfort to those near and dear to him, and to the world at large, as well as provide for his own intellectual welfare; whereas before, however kind his treatment, all his earnings more than his expenses went to enrich his master. It is on this account, probably, that those who have undertaken to carry out some principles of humanity in their treatment of their slaves, have been generally frowned upon by their neighbors; and they have been forced either to emancipate their slaves, or to return to the cruel practices of those around them. My young master preferred the former alternative; my old master adopted the latter. We now began to taste a little of the horrors of slavery; so that many of the slaves ran away, which had not been the case before. My master employed an overseer also, about this time, which he always refused to do previously, preferring to take charge of us himself; but the clamor of the neighbors was so great at his mild treatment of his slaves, that he at length yielded to the popular will around him, and went "with the multitude to do evil," and hired an overseer. This was an end of our favorable treatment; and there is no telling what would have been the result of this new method among slaves so unused to the whip as we were, if in the midst of this experiment, old master had not been called upon to pay "the debt of nature," and to "go the way of all the earth." As he was about to expire, he sent for me and my brother, to come to his bedside. We ran with beating hearts, and highly elated feelings, not doubting that he was about to confer upon us the boon of freedom, as we expected to be set free when he died; but imagine my deep disappointment, when the old man called me to his side and said to me, "Henry, you will make a good plough-boy, or a good gardener; now you must be an honest boy, and never tell an untruth. I have given you to my son William, and you must obey him." Thus did this old gentleman deceive us by his former kind treatment, and raise expectations in our youthful minds, which were thus doomed to be fatally overthrown. Poor man! he has gone to a higher tribunal than man's, and doubtless ere this, earnestly laments that he did not give us all our liberty at this favorable moment; but sad as was our disappointment, we were constrained to submit to it, as we best were able. One old negro openly expressed his wish that master would die, because he had not released him from his bondage.

If there is any one thing which operates as an impetus to the slave in his toilsome labors and buoys him up, under all the hardships of his severe lot, it is this hope of future freedom, which lights up his soul and cheers his desolate heart in the midst of all the fearful agonies of the varied scenes of his slave life, as the soul of the tempest-tossed mariner is stayed from complete despair, by the faint glimmering of the far-distant light which the kindness of man has placed in a lighthouse, so as to be perceived by him at a long distance. Old ocean's tempestuous waves beat and roar against his frail bark, and the briny deep seems ready to enclose him in its wide open mouth, but "ever and anon" he perceives the glimmering of this feeble light in the distance, which keeps alive the spark of hope in his bosom, which kind heaven has placed within every man's breast. So with the slave. Freedom's fires are dimly burning in the far distant future, and ever and anon a fresh flame appears to arise in the direction of this sacred altar, until at times it seems to approach so near, that he can feel its melting power dissolving his chains, and causing him to emerge from his darkened prison, into the full light of freedom's glorious liberty. O the fond anticipations of the slave in this respect! I cannot correctly describe them to you, but I can recollect the thrills of exulting joy which the name of freedom caused to flow through my soul. Freedom, the dear and joyful sound, 'Tis music in the sad slave's ear. How often this hope is destined to fade away, as the early dew before the rising sun! Not unseldom, does the slave labor intensely to obtain the means to purchase his freedom, and after having paid the required sum, is still held a slave, while the master retains the money! This very often transpires under the slave system. A good many slaves have in this way paid for themselves several times, and not received their freedom then! And masters often hold out this inducement to their slaves, to labor more than they otherwise would, when they have no intention of fulfilling their promise. O the ineffable meanness of the slave system! Instead of our being set free, a far different fate awaited us; and here you behold, reader, the closing scene of the kindest treatment which a man can bestow upon his slaves.

It mattered not how benign might have been our master's conduct to us, it was to be succeeded by a harrowing scene, the inevitable consequence of our being left slaves. We must now be separated and divided into different lots, as we were inherited by the four sons of my master. It is no easy matter to amicably divide even the old furniture and worn-out implements of husbandry, and sometimes the very clothing of a deceased person, and oftentimes a scene of shame ensues at the opening of the will of a departed parent, which is enough to cause humanity to blush at the meanness of man. What then must be the sufferings of those persons, who are to be the objects of this division and strife? See the heirs of a departed slaveholder, disputing as to the rightful possession of human beings, many of them their old nurses, and their playmates in their younger days! The scene which took place at the division of my master's human property, baffles all description. I was then only thirteen years of age, but it is as fresh in my mind as if but yesterday's sun had shone upon the dreadful exhibition. My mother was separated from her youngest child, and not until she had begged and pleaded most piteously for its restoration to her, was it again placed in her hands. Turning her eyes fondly upon me, who was now to be carried from her presence, she said, "You now see, my son, the fulfilment of what I told you a great while ago, when I used to take you on my knee, and show you the leaves blown from the trees by the fearful winds." Yes, I now saw that one after another were the slave mother's children torn from her embrace, and John was given to one brother, Sarah to another, and Jane to a third, while Samuel fell into the hands of the fourth. It is a difficult matter to satisfactorily divide the slaves on a plantation, for no person wishes for all children, or for all old people; while both old, young, and middle-aged ones are to be divided. There is no equitable way of dividing them, but by allowing each one to take his portion of both children, middle aged and old people; which necessarily causes heart-rending separations; but "slaves have no feelings," I am sometimes told. "You get used to these things; it would not do for us to experience them, but you are not constituted as we are;" to which I reply, that a slave's friends are all he possesses that is of value to him. He cannot read, he has no property, he cannot be a teacher of truth, or a politician; he cannot be very religious, and all that remains to him, aside from the hope of freedom, that ever-present deity, forever inspiring him in his most terrible hours of despair, is the society of his friends. We love our friends more than white people love theirs, for we risk more to save them from suffering. Many of our number who have escaped from bondage ourselves, have jeopardized our own liberty, in order to release our friends, and sometimes we have been retaken and made slaves of again, while endeavoring to rescue our friends from slavery's iron jaws.

But does not the slave love his friends! What mean then those frantic screams, which every slave-auction witnesses, where the scalding tears rush in agonizing torrents down the sorrow-stricken cheeks of the bereaved slave mother; and where clubs are sometimes used to drive apart two fond friends who cling to each other, as the merciless slave-trader is to separate them forever. O, to talk of our not having feelings for our friends, is to mock that Being who has created us in his own image, and implanted deep in every human bosom, a gushing fount of tender sensibilities, which no life of sin can ever fully erase. Talk of our not having feelings, and then calmly look on the scene described as taking place when my master died! Have you any feeling? Does this recital arouse those sympathetic feelings in your bosom which you make your boast of? How can white people have hearts of tenderness, and allow such scenes to daily transpire at the South? All over the blackened and marred surface of the whole slave territory do these heart-rending transactions continually occur. Not a day inscribes its departing hours upon the dial of human existence, but it marks the overthrow of more than one family altar, and the sundering of numerous family ties; and yet the hot blood of Southern oppression is allowed to find its way into the hearts of the Northern people, who politically and religiously are doing their utmost to sustain the dreadful system; yea, competing with the South in their devotion to the evil genius of their country's choice. Slavery reigns and rules the councils of this nation, as Satan presides over Pandemonium, and the loud and clear cry of the anti-slavery host, calling upon the people of the land to cease their connection with the tyrannical system, is universally unheeded. It falls upon the closed ears of the people of this nation like the noise of the random shots of a vessel at sea, upon the ears of the captain of the opposing squadron, but to arouse them to action in opposition to the utterance of the voice of warning.

What though the plaintive cries of three millions of heart-broken and dejected captives, are wafted on every Southern gale to the ears of our Northern brethren, and the hot winds of the South reach our fastnesses amid the mountains and hills of our rugged land, loaded with the stifled cries and choking sobs of poor desolate woman, as her babes are torn one by one from her embrace; yet no Northern voice is heard to sound loudly enough among our hills and dales, to startle from their sleep of indifference, those who have it in their power to break the chains of the suffering bondmen to-day, saying to all who hear its clear sounding voice, "Come out from all connection with this terrible system of cruelty and blood, and form a government and a union free from this hateful curse." The Northern people have it in their power to-day, to cause all this suffering of which I have been speaking to cease, and to cause one loud and triumphant anthem of praise to ascend from the millions of panting, bleeding slaves, now stretched upon the plains of Southern oppression; and yet they talk of our being destitute of feeling. "O shame, where is thy blush!"

My father and mother were left on the plantation, and I was taken to the city of Richmond, to work in a tobacco manufactory, owned by my master's son William, who now became my only master. Old master, although he did not give me my freedom, yet left an especial charge with his son to take good care of me, and not to whip me, which charge my master endeavored to act in accordance with. He told me if I would behave well he would take good care of me, and would give me money to spend, &c. He talked so kindly to me that I determined I would exert myself to the utmost to please him, and would endeavor to do just what he wished me to, in every respect. He furnished me with a new suit of clothes, and gave me money to buy things with, to send to my mother. One day I overheard him telling the overseer that his father had raised me, and that I was a smart boy, and he must never whip me. I tried extremely hard to perform what I thought was my duty, and escaped the lash almost entirely; although the overseer would oftentimes have liked to have given me a severe whipping; but fear of both me and my master deterred him from so doing. It is true, my lot was still comparatively easy; but reader, imagine not that others were so fortunate as myself, as I will presently describe to you the character of our overseer; and you can judge what kind of treatment, persons wholly in his power might expect from such a man. But it was some time before I became reconciled to my fate, for after being so constantly with my mother, to be torn from her side, and she on a distant plantation, where I could not see or but seldom hear from her, was exceedingly trying to my youthful feelings, slave though I was. I missed her smiling look when her eye rested upon my form; and when I returned from my daily toil, weary and dejected, no fond mother's arms were extended to meet me, no one appeared to sympathize with me, and I felt I was indeed alone in the world. After the lapse of about a year and a half from the time I commenced living in Richmond, a strange series of events transpired. I did not then know precisely what was the cause of these scenes, for I could not get any very satisfactory information concerning the matter from my master, only that some of the slaves had undertaken to kill their owners; but I have since learned that it was the famous Nat Turner's insurrection that caused all the excitement I witnessed. Slaves were whipped, hung, and cut down with swords in the streets, if found away from their quarters after dark. The whole city was in the utmost confusion and dismay; and a dark cloud of terrific blackness, seemed to hang over the heads of the whites. So true is it, that "the wicked flee when no man pursueth." Great numbers of the slaves were locked in the prison, and many were "half hung," as it was termed; that is, they were suspended to some limb of a tree, with a rope about their necks, so adjusted as not to quite strangle them, and then they were pelted by the men and boys with rotten eggs. This half-hanging is a refined species of cruelty, peculiar to slavery, I believe.

Among the cruelties occasioned by this insurrection, which was however some distance from Richmond, was the forbidding of as many as five slaves to meet together, except they were at work, and the silencing of all colored preachers. One of that class in our city, refused to obey the imperial mandate, and was severely whipped; but his religion was too deeply rooted to be thus driven from him, and no promise could be extorted from his resolute soul, that he would not proclaim what he considered the glad tidings of the gospel. (Query. How many white preachers would continue their employment, if they were served in the same way?) It is strange that more insurrections do not take place among the slaves; but their masters have impressed upon their minds so forcibly the fact, that the United States Government is pledged to put them down, in case they should attempt any such movement, that they have no heart to contend against such fearful odds; and yet the slaveholder lives in constant dread of such an event.[3]

The rustling of "—— —— —— the lightest leaf, That quivers to the passing breeze," fills his timid soul with visions of flowing blood and burning dwellings; and as the loud thunder of heaven rolls over his head, and the vivid lightning flashes across his pale face, straightway his imagination conjures up terrible scenes of the loud roaring of an enemy's cannon, and the fierce yells of an infuriated slave population, rushing to vengeance.[4] There is no doubt but this would be the case, if it were not for the Northern people, who are ready, as I have been often told, to shoot us down, if we attempt to rise and obtain our freedom. I believe that if the slaves could do as they wish, they would throw off their heavy yoke immediately, by rising against their masters; but ten millions of Northern people stand with their feet on their necks, and how can they arise? How was Nat Turner's insurrection suppressed, but by a company of United States troops, furnished the governor of Virginia at his request, according to your Constitution?

About this time, I began to grow alarmed respecting my future welfare, as a great eclipse of the sun had recently taken place; and the cholera reaching the country not long after, I thought that perhaps the day of judgment was not far distant, and I must prepare for that dreaded event. After praying for about three months, it pleased Almighty God, as I believe, to pardon my sins, and I was received into the Baptist Church, by a minister who thought it was wicked to hold slaves. I was obliged to obtain permission from my master, however, before I could join. He gave me a note to carry to the preacher, saying that I had his permission to join the church!

I shall now make you acquainted with the manner in which affairs were conducted in my master's tobacco manufactory, after which I shall introduce you to the heart-rending scenes which give the principal interest to my narrative.

My master carried on a large tobacco manufacturing establishment in Richmond, which was almost wholly under the supervision of one of those low, miserable, cruel, barbarous, and sometimes religious beings, known under the name of overseers, with which the South abounds. These men hardly deserve the name of men, for they are lost to all regard for decency, truth, justice and humanity, and are so far gone in human depravity, that before they can be saved, Jesus Christ, or some other Saviour, will have to die a second time. I pity them sincerely, but as my mind recurs to the wicked conduct I so often witnessed on the part of this one, I cannot prevent these indignant feelings from arising in my soul. O reader, if you had seen the perfect recklessness of conduct so often exhibited by this man, as I witnessed it, you would not blame me for expressing myself so strongly. I know that even this man is my brother, but he is a very wicked brother, whose soul I commend to Almighty God, hoping that his sovereign grace may find its way, if it is a possible thing, to his sin-hardened soul; and yet he was a pious man. His name was John F. Allen, and I suppose he still lives in Richmond. After reading about his character, I apprehend your judgment of him will coincide with mine. The other overseers, however, were very different men, for hell could hardly spare more than one such man, for one tobacco manufactory; as it is not overstocked with such vile reprobates.

But before proceeding to speak farther of him, I will inform you a little respecting our business—as not many of you have ever seen the inside of a tobacco manufactory. The building I worked in was about 300 feet in length, and three stories high, and afforded room for 200 people to work in, but only 150 persons were employed, 120 of whom were slaves, and the remainder free colored people. We were obliged to work fourteen hours a day, in the summer, and sixteen in the winter.

This work consisted in removing the stems from the leaves of tobacco, which was performed by women and boys, after which the tobacco was moistened with a liquor made from liquorice and sugar, which gives the tobacco that sweetish taste which renders it not perfectly abhorrent to those who chew it. After being thus moistened, the tobacco was taken by the men and twisted into hands, and pressed into lumps, when it was sent to the machine-house, and pressed into boxes and casks. After remaining in what was called the "sweat-house" about thirty days, it was shipped for the market.

Mr. Allen was a thorough going Yankee in his mode of doing business. He was by no means one of your indolent, do-nothing Southerners, so effeminate as to be hardly able to wield his hands to administer to his own necessities, but he was a savage-looking, dare-devil sort of a man, ready apparently for any emergency to which

Beelzebub might call him, a real servant of the bottomless pit. He understood how to turn a penny as well as any Yankee pedlar who ever visited our city. Whether he derived his skill from associating with that class of individuals, or whether it was the natural production of his own cunning mind, I know not. He used often to boast, that by his shrewdness in managing the negroes, he made enough to support his family, which cost him $1000, without touching a farthing of his salary, which was $1500 per annum. Of the probability of this assertion, I can bear witness; for I know he was very skilful in another department of cunning and cheatery. Like many other servants of the evil one, he was an early riser; not for the purpose of improving his health, or that he might enjoy sweet communion with his heavenly Father, at his morning orisons, but that "while the master slept" he might more easily transact his nefarious business. At whatever hour of the morning I might arrive at the factory, I seldom anticipated the seemingly industrious steps of Mr. Allen, who by his punctuality in this respect, obtained a good reputation as a faithful and devoted overseer. But mark the conduct of the pious gentleman, for he was a member of an Episcopalian church. One would have supposed from observing the transactions around him, that Mr. Allen took time by the forelock, emphatically, for long before the early rays of the rising sun had gilded the eastern horizon, was this man busily engaged in loading a wagon with coal, oil, sugar, wood, &c., &c., which always found a place of deposit at his own door, entirely unknown to my master. This practice Mr. Allen carried on during my stay there, and yet he was a very pious man.

This man enjoyed the unlimited confidence of my master, so that he would never listen to a word of complaint on the part of any of the workmen. No matter how cruel or how unjust might be the punishment inflicted upon any of the hands, master would never listen to their complaints; so that this barbarous man was our master in reality. At one time a colored man, who had been in the habit of singing religious songs quite often, was taken sick and did not make his appearance at the factory. For two or three days no notice whatever was taken of him, no medicine provided for him, and no physician sent to heal him. At the end of that time, Mr. Allen ordered three strong men to go to the man's house, and bring him to the factory. This order being obeyed, the man, pale and hardly able to stand, was stripped to his waist, his hands tied together, and the rope fastened to a large post. The overseer then questioned him about his singing, told him that it consumed too much time, and that he was going to give him some medicine which would cure him. The poor trembling man made no reply, when the pious Mr. Allen, for no crime except that of sickness, inflicted 200 lashes upon the quivering flesh of the invalid, and he would have continued his "apostolic blows," if the emaciated form of the languishing man, had not sunken under their heavy weight, and Mr. Allen was obliged to desist.[5] I witnessed this transaction with my own eyes; but what could I do, for I was a slave, and any interference on my part would only have brought the same punishment upon me. This man was sick a month afterwards, during which time the weekly allowance of seventy-five cents for the hands to board themselves with, was withheld from him, and his wife was obliged to support him by washing for others; and yet Northern people tell me that a slave is better off than a free man, because when he is sick his master provides for him! Master knew all the circumstances of this case, but never uttered one word of reproof to the overseer, that I could learn; at any rate, he did not interfere at all with this cruel treatment of him, as his motto was, "Mr. Allen is always right."

Mr. Allen, although a church member, was much addicted to the habit of profane swearing, a vice which church members there, indulged in as frequently as non-professors did. He used particularly to expend his swearing breath, in denunciation of the whole race of negroes, calling us "d——d hogs, dogs, pigs," &c. At one time, he was busily engaged in reading in the Bible, when a slave came in who had absented himself from work the enormous length of ten minutes! The overseer had been cheated out of ten minutes' precious time; and as he depended upon the punctuality of the slave to support his family in the manner mentioned previously, his desire perhaps not to violate that precept, "he that provideth not for his family is worse than an infidel," led him to indulge in quite an outbreak of boisterous anger. "What are you so late for, you black scamp?" said he to the delinquent. "I am only ten minutes behind the time, sir," quietly responded the slave, when Mr. Allen exclaimed, "You are a d———d liar," and remembering, for aught that I can say to the contrary, that "he that converteth a sinner from the error of his ways, shall save a soul from death," he proceeded to try the effect of the Bible upon the body of the "liar," striking him a heavy blow in the face, with the sacred book. But that not answering his purpose, and the man remaining incorrigible, he caught up a stick and beat him with that. The slave complained to master, but he would take no notice of him, and directed him back to the overseer.

Mr. Allen, although a superintendent of the Sabbath school, and very fervid in his exhortations to the slave children, whom he endeavored to instruct in reference to their duties to their masters, that they must never disobey them, or lie, or steal, and if they did they would assuredly "go to hell," yet was not wholly destitute of "that fear which hath torment," for always when a heavy thunder storm came up, would he shut himself up in a little room where he supposed the lightning would not harm him; and I frequently overheard him praying earnestly to God to spare his life. He evidently had not that "perfect love which casteth out fear." The same day on which he had beaten the poor sick man, did such a scene transpire; but generally after the storm had abated he would laugh at his own conduct, and say he did not believe the Lord had any thing to do with the thunder and lightning.

As I have stated, Mr. A. was a devout attendant upon public worship, and prayed much with the pupils in the Sabbath school, and was indefatigable in teaching them to repeat the catechism after him, although he was very particular never to allow them to hold the book in their hands. But let not my readers suppose on this account, that he desired the salvation of these slaves. No, far from that; for very soon after thus exhorting them, he would tell his visiters, that it was "a d——d lie that colored people were ever converted," and that they could "not go to heaven," for they had no souls; but that it was his duty to talk to them as he did. The reader can learn from this account of how much value the religious teaching of the slaves is, when such men are its administerers; and also for what purpose this instruction is given them.

This man's liberality to white people, was coextensive with his denunciation of the colored race. A white man, he said, could not be lost, let him do what he pleased—rob the slaves, which he said was not wrong, lie, swear, or any thing else, provided he read the Bible and joined the Church.[6]

One word concerning the religion of the South. I regard it as all delusion, and that there is not a particle of religion in their slaveholding churches. The great end to which religion is there made to minister, is to keep the slaves in a docile and submissive frame of mind, by instilling into them the idea that if they do not obey their masters, they will infallibly "go to hell;" and yet some of the miserable wretches who teach this doctrine, do not themselves believe it. Of course the slave prefers obedience to his master, to an abode in the "lake of fire and brimstone." It is true in more senses than one, that slavery rests upon hell! I once heard a minister declare in public, that he had preached six years before he was converted; and that he was then in the habit of taking a glass of "mint julep" directly after prayers, which wonderfully refreshed him, soul and body. This dram he would repeat three or four times during the day;

but at length an old slave persuaded him to abstain a while from his potations, the following of which advice, resulted in his conversion. I believe his second conversion, was nearer a true one, than his first, because he said his conscience reproved him for having sold slaves; and he finally left that part of the country, on account of slavery, and went to the North.

But as time passed along, I began to think seriously of entering into the matrimonial state, as much as a person can, who can "make no contract whatever," and whose wife is not his, only so far as her master allows her to be. I formed an acquaintance with a young woman by the name of Nancy—belonging to a Mr. Lee, a clerk in the bank, and a pious man; and our friendship having ripened into mutual love, we concluded to make application to the powers that ruled us, for permission to be married, as I had previously applied for permission to join the church. I went to Mr. Lee, and made known to him my wishes, when he told me, he never meant to sell Nancy, and if my master would agree never to sell me, then I might marry her. This man was a member of a Presbyterian church in Richmond, and pretended to me, to believe it wrong to separate families; but after I had been married to my wife one year, his conscientious scruples vanished, and she was sold to a saddler living in Richmond, who was one of Dr. Plummer's church members. Mr. Lee gave me a note to my master, and they afterwards discussed the matter over, and I was allowed to marry the chosen one of my heart. Mr. Lee, as I have said, soon sold my wife, contrary to his promise, and she fell into the hands of a very cruel mistress, the wife of the saddler above mentioned, by whom she was much abused. This woman used to wish for some great calamity to happen to my wife, because she stayed so long when she went to nurse her child; which calamity came very near happening afterwards to herself. My wife was finally sold, on account of the solicitations of this woman; but four months had hardly elapsed, before she insisted upon her being purchased back again.

During all this time, my mind was in a continual agitation, for I knew not one day, who would be the owner of my wife the next. O reader, have you no heart to sympathize with the injured slave, as he thus lives in a state of perpetual torment, the dread uncertainty of his wife's fate, continually hanging over his head, and poisoning all his joys, as the naked sword hung by a hair, over the head of an ancient king's guest, as he was seated at a table loaded with all the luxuries of an epicure's devising? This sword, unlike the one alluded to, did often pierce my breast, and when I had recovered from the wound, it was again hung up, to torture me. This is slavery, a natural and concomitant part of the accursed system!

The saddler who owned my wife, whose name I suppress for particular reasons, was at one time taken sick, but when his minister, the Rev. (so called) Dr. Plummer came to pray with him, he would not allow him to perform that rite, which strengthened me in the opinion I entertained of Dr. Plummer, that he was as wicked a man as this saddler, and you will presently see, how bad a man he was. The saddler sent for his slaves to pray for him, and afterwards for me, and when I repaired to his bed-side, he beseeched me to pray for him, saying that he would live a much better life than he had done, if the Lord would only spare him. I and the other slaves prayed three nights for him, after our work was over, and we needed rest in sleep; but the earnest desire of this man, induced us to forego our necessary rest; and yet one of the first things he did after his recovery, was to sell my wife. When he was reminded of my praying for his restoration to health, he angrily exclaimed, that it was "all d——d lies" about the Lord restoring him to health in consequence of the negroes praying for him,—and that if any of them mentioned that they had prayed for him, he "would whip them for it."

The last purchaser of my wife, was Mr. Samuel S. Cartrell, also a member of Dr. Plummer's church.[7] He induced me to pay him $50,00 in order to assist him in purchasing my companion, so as to prevent her being sold away from me. I also paid him $50 a year, for her time, although she would have been of but little value to him, for she had young children and could not earn much for him,—and rented a house for which I paid $72, and she took in washing, which with the remainder of my earnings, after deducting master's "lion's share," supported our family. Our bliss, as far as the term bliss applies to a slave's situation, was now complete in this respect, for a season; for never had we been so pleasantly situated before; but, reader, behold its cruel termination. O the harrowing remembrance of those terrible, terrible scenes! May God spare you from ever enduring what I then endured.

It was on a pleasant morning, in the month of August, 1848, that I left my wife and three children safely at our little home, and proceeded to my allotted labor. The sun shone brightly as he commenced his daily task, and as I gazed upon his early rays, emitting their golden light upon the rich fields adjacent to the city, and glancing across the abode of my wife and family, and as I beheld the numerous companies of slaves, hieing their way to their daily labors, and reflected upon the difference between their lot and mine, I felt that, although I was a slave, there were many alleviations to my cup of sorrow. It was true, that the greater portion of my earnings was taken from me, by the unscrupulous hands of my dishonest master,—that I was entirely at his mercy, and might at any hour be snatched from what sources of joy were open to me—that he might, if he chose, extend his robber hand, and demand a still larger portion of my earnings,—and above all, that intellectual privileges were entirely denied me; but as I imprinted a parting kiss upon the lips of my faithful wife, and pressed to my bosom the little darling cherubs, who followed me saying, in their childish accents, "Father, come back soon," I felt that life was not all a blank to me; that there were some pure joys yet my portion. O, how my heart would have been riven with unutterable anguish, if I had then realized the awful calamity which was about to burst upon my unprotected head! Reader, are you a husband, and can you listen to my sad story, without being moved to cease all your connection with that stern power, which stretched out its piratical arm, and basely robbed me of all dear to me on earth!

The sun had traced his way to mid-heaven, and the hour for the laborers to turn from their tasks, and to seek refreshment for their toil-worn frames,—and when I should take my prattling children on my knee,—was fast approaching; but there burst upon me a sound so dreadful, and so sudden, that the shock well nigh overwhelmed me. It was as if the heavens themselves had fallen upon me, and the everlasting hills of God's erecting, like an avalanche, had come rolling over my head! And what was it? "Your wife and smiling babes are gone; in prison they are locked, and to-morrow's sun will see them far away from you, on their way to the distant South!" Pardon the utterance of my feelings here, reader, for surely a man may feel, when all that he prizes on earth is, at one fell stroke, swept from his reach! O God, if there is a moment when vengeance from thy righteous throne should be hurled upon guilty man, and hot thunderbolts of wrath, should burst upon his wicked head, it surely is at such a time as this! And this is Slavery; its certain, necessary and constituent part. Without this terrific pillar to its demon walls, it falls to the ground, as a bridge sinks, when its buttresses are swept from under it by the rushing floods. This is Slavery. No kind master's indulgent care can guard his chosen slave, his petted chattel, however fond he may profess to be of such a piece of property, from so fearful a calamity. My master treated me as kindly as he could, and retain me in slavery; but did that keep me from experiencing this terrible deprivation? The sequel will show you even his care for me. What could I do? I had left my fond wife and prattling children, as happy as slaves could expect to be; as I was not anticipating their loss, for the pious man who bought them last, had, as you recollect, received a sum of money from me, under the promise of not selling them. My first impulse, of course, was to rush to the jail, and behold my family once more, before our final separation. I started for this infernal place, but had not proceeded a great distance, before I met a gentleman, who stopped me, and beholding my anguish of heart, as depicted on my countenance, inquired of me what the trouble was with me. I told him as I best could, when he advised me not to go to the jail, for the man who had sold my wife, had told my master some falsehoods about me, and had induced him to give orders to the jailor to seize me, and confine me in prison, if I should appear there. He said I would undoubtedly be sold separate from my wife, and he thought I had better not go there. I then persuaded a young man of my acquaintance to go to the prison, and sent by him, to my wife, some money and a message in reference to the cause of my failure to visit her. It seems that it would have been useless for me to have ventured there, for as soon as this young man arrived, and inquired for my wife, he was seized and put in prison,—the jailor mistaking him for me; but when he discovered his mistake, he was very angry, and vented his rage upon the innocent youth, by kicking him out of prison. I then repaired to my Christian master, and there several times, during the ensuing twenty-four hours, did I beseech and entreat him to purchase my wife; but no tears of mine made the least impression upon his obdurate heart. I laid my case before him, and reminded him of the faithfulness with which I had served him, and of my utmost endeavors to please him, but this kind master—recollect reader—utterly refused to advance a small portion of the $5,000 I had paid him, in order to relieve my sufferings; and he was a member, in good and regular standing, of an Episcopal church in Richmond! His reply to me was worthy of the morality of Slavery, and shows just how much religion, the kindest and most pious of Southern slaveholders have. "You can get another wife," said he; but I told him the Bible said, "What God has joined together, let not man put asunder," and that I did not want any other wife but my own lawful one, whom I loved so much. At the mention of this passage of Scripture, he drove me from his house, saying, he did not wish to hear that!

I now endeavored to persuade two gentlemen of my acquaintance, to buy my wife; but they told me they did not think it was right to hold slaves, or else they would gladly assist me, for they sincerely pitied me, and advised me to go to my master again; but I knew this would be useless. My agony was now complete. She with whom I had travelled the journey of life, for the space of twelve years, with three little pledges of domestic affection, must now be forever separated from me—I must remain alone and desolate. O God, shall my wife and children never more greet my sight, with their cheerful looks and happy smiles? Far, far away, in Carolina's swamps are they now, toiling beneath the scorching rays of the hot sun, with no husband's voice to soothe the hardships of my wife's lot, and no father's kind look to gladden the heart of my disconsolate little ones.[8]

I call upon you, Sons of the North, if your blood has not lost its bright color of liberty, and is not turned to the blackened gore which surrounds the slaveholder's polluted hearts, to arise in your might, and demand the liberation of the slaves. If you do not, at the day of final account, I shall bear witness against you, as well as against the slaveholders themselves, as the cause of my and my brethren's bereavement. Think you, at that dread hour, you can escape the scrutinizing look of the Judge of all the earth, as he "maketh inquisition for the blood of the innocents?" Oh, no; but equally with the Southern slaveholders, will your character be condemned by the Ruler of the universe.

The next day, I stationed myself by the side of the road, along which the slaves, amounting to three hundred and fifty, were to pass. The purchaser of my wife was a Methodist minister, who was about starting for North Carolina. Pretty soon five waggonloads of little children passed, and looking at the foremost one, what should I see but a little child, pointing its tiny hand towards me, exclaiming, "There's my father; I knew he would come and bid me good-bye." It was my eldest child! Soon the gang approached in which my wife was chained. I looked, and beheld her familiar face; but O, reader, that glance of agony! may God spare me ever again enduring the excruciating horror of that moment! She passed, and came near to where I stood. I seized hold of her hand, intending to bid her farewell; but words failed me; the gift of utterance had fled, and I remained speechless. I followed her for some distance, with her hand grasped in mine, as if to save her from her fate, but I could not speak, and I was obliged to turn away in silence.

This is not an imaginary scene, reader; it is not a fiction, but an every-day reality at the South; and all I can say more to you, in reference to it is, that if you will not, after being made acquainted with these facts, consecrate your all to the slaves' release from bondage, you are utterly unworthy the name of a man, and should go and hide yourself, in some impenetrable cave, where no eye can behold your demon form.

One more scene occurs in the tragical history of my life, before the curtain drops, and I retire from the stage of observation, as far as past events are concerned; not, however, to shrink from public gaze, as if ashamed of my perilous adventures, or to retire into private life, lest the bloodhounds of the South should scent my steps, and start in pursuit of their missing property. No, reader, for as long as three millions of my countrymen pine in cruel bondage, on Virginia's exhausted soil, and in Carolina's pestilential rice swamps; in the cane-breaks of Georgia, and on the cotton fields of Louisiana and Mississippi, and in the insalubrious climate of Texas; as well as suffer under the slave-driver's cruel lash, all over the almost God-forsaken South; I shall never refuse to advocate their claims to your sympathy, whenever a fitting occasion occurs to speak in their behalf.

But you are eager to learn the particulars of my journey from freedom to liberty. The first thing that occurred to me, after the cruel separation of my wife and children from me, and I had recovered my senses, so as to know how to act, was, thoughts of freeing myself from slavery's iron yoke. I had suffered enough under its heavy weight, and I determined I would endure it no longer; and those reasons which often deter the slave from attempting to escape, no longer existed in reference to me, for my family were gone, and slavery now had no mitigating circumstances, to lessen the bitterness of its cup of woe. It is true, as my master had told me, that I could "get another wife;" but no man, excepting a brute below the human species, would have proposed such a step to a person in my circumstances; and as I was not such a degraded being, I did not dream of so conducting. Marriage was not a thing of personal convenience with me, to be cast aside as a worthless garment, whenever the slaveholder's will required it; but it was a sacred institution binding upon me, as long as the God who had "joined us together," refrained from untying the nuptial knot. What! leave the wife of my bosom for another! and while my heart was leaping from its abode, to pour its strong affections upon the kindred soul of my devoted partner, could I receive a stranger, another person to my embrace, as if the ties of love existed only in the presence of the object loved! Then, indeed, should I have been a traitor to that God, who had linked our hearts together in fond affection, and cemented our union, by so many additional cords, twining around our hearts; as a tree and an arbor are held together by the clinging of the tendrils of the adhering vine, which winds itself about them so closely. Slavery, and slavery abettors, seize hold of these tender scions, and cut and prune them away from both tree and arbor, as remorselessly as a gardener cuts down the briars and thorns which disturb the growth of his fair plants; but all humane, and every virtuous man, must instinctively recoil from such transactions, as they would from soul murder, or from the commission of some enormous deed of villany.

Reader, in the light of these scenes you may behold, as in a glass, your true character. Refined and delicate you may pretend to be, and may pass yourself off as a pure and virtuous person; but if you refuse to exert yourself for the overthrow of a system, which thus tramples human affection under its bloody feet, and demands of its crushed victims, the sacrifice of all that is noble, virtuous and pure, upon its smoking altars; you may rest assured, that if the balances of purity were extended before you, He who "searcheth the hearts, and trieth the reins," would say to you, as your character underwent his searching scrutiny, "Thou art weighed in the balance and found wanting."

I went to Mr. Allen, and requested of him permission to refrain from labor for a short time, in consequence of a disabled finger; but he refused to grant me this permission, on the ground that my hand was not lame enough to justify him in so doing. Nothing daunted by this rebuff, I took some oil of vitriol, intending to pour a few drops upon my finger, to make it sufficiently sore, to disable me from work, which I succeeded in, beyond my wishes; for in my hurry, a larger quantity than it was my purpose to apply to my finger, found its way there, and my finger was soon eaten through to the bone. The overseer then was obliged to allow me to absent myself from business, for it was impossible for me to work in that situation. But I did not waste my precious furlough in idle mourning over my fate. I armed myself with determined energy, for action, and in the words of one of old, in the name of God, "I leaped over a wall, and run through a troop" of difficulties. After searching for assistance for some time, I at length was so fortunate as to find a friend, who promised to assist me, for one half the money I had about me, which was one hundred and sixty-six dollars. I gave him eighty-six, and he was to do his best in forwarding my scheme. Long did we remain together, attempting to devise ways and means to carry me away from the land of separation of families, of whips and thumbscrews, and auction blocks; but as often as a plan was suggested by my friend, there would appear some difficulty in the way of its accomplishment. Perhaps it may not be best to mention what these plans were, as some unfortunate slaves may thereby be prevented from availing themselves of these methods of escape.

At length, after praying earnestly to Him, who seeth afar off, for assistance, in my difficulty, suddenly, as if from above, there darted into my mind these words, "Go and get a box, and put yourself in it." I pondered the words over in my mind. "Get a box?" thought I; "what can this mean?" But I was "not disobedient unto the heavenly vision," and I determined to put into practice this direction, as I considered it, from my heavenly Father.[9] I went to the depot, and there noticed the size of the largest boxes, which commonly were sent by the cars, and returned with their dimensions. I then repaired to a carpenter, and induced him to make me a box of such a description as I wished, informing him of the use I intended to make of it. He assured me I could not live in it; but as it was dear liberty I was in pursuit of, I thought it best to make the trial.

When the box was finished, I carried it, and placed it before my friend, who had promised to assist me, who asked me if that was to "put my clothes in?" I replied that it was not, but to "put Henry Brown in!" He was astonished at my temerity; but I insisted upon his placing me in it, and nailing me up, and he finally consented.

After corresponding with a friend in Philadelphia, arrangements were made for my departure, and I took my place in this narrow prison, with a mind full of uncertainty as to the result. It was a critical period of my life, I can assure you, reader; but if you have never been deprived of your liberty, as I was, you cannot realize the power of that hope of freedom, which was to me indeed, "an anchor to the soul, both sure and steadfast."

I laid me down in my darkened home of three feet by two, and like one about to be guillotined, resigned myself to my fate. My friend was to accompany me, but he failed to do so; and contented himself with sending a telegraph message to his correspondent in Philadelphia, that such a box was on its way to his care.

I took with me a bladder filled with water to bathe my neck with, in case of too great heat; and with no access to the fresh air, excepting three small gimblet holes, I started on my perilous cruise. I was first carried to the express office, the box being placed on its end, so that I started with my head downwards, although the box was directed, "this side up with care." From the express office, I was carried to the depot, and from thence tumbled roughly into the baggage car, where I happened to fall "right side up," but no thanks to my transporters. But after a while the cars stopped, and I was put aboard a steamboat, and placed on my head. In this dreadful position, I remained the space of an hour and a half, it seemed to me, when I began to feel of my eyes and head, and found to my dismay, that my eyes were almost swollen out of their sockets, and the veins on my temple seemed ready to burst. I made no noise however, determining to obtain "victory or death," but endured the terrible pain, as well as I could, sustained under the whole by the thoughts of sweet liberty. About half an hour afterwards, I attempted again to lift my hands to my face, but I found I was not able to move them. A cold sweat now covered me from head to foot. Death seemed my inevitable fate, and every moment I expected to feel the blood flowing over me, which had burst from my veins. One half hour longer and my sufferings would have ended in that fate, which I preferred to slavery; but I lifted up my heart to God in prayer, believing that he would yet deliver me, when to my joy, I overheard two men say, "We have been here two hours and have travelled twenty miles, now let us sit down, and rest ourselves." They suited the action to the word, and turned the box over, containing my soul and body, thus delivering me from the power of the grim messenger of death, who a few moments previously, had aimed his fatal shaft at my head, and had placed his icy hands on my throbbing heart. One of these men inquired of the other, what he supposed that box contained, to which his comrade replied, that he guessed it was the mail. "Yes," thought I, "it is a male, indeed, although not the mail of the United States."

Soon after this fortunate event, we arrived at Washington, where I was thrown from the wagon, and again as my luck would have it, fell on my head. I was then rolled down a declivity, until I reached the platform from which the cars were to start. During this short but rapid journey, my neck came very near being dislocated, as I felt it crack, as if it had snapped asunder. Pretty soon, I heard some one say, "there is no room for this box, it will have to remain behind." I then again applied to the Lord, my help in all my difficulties, and in a few minutes I heard a gentleman direct the hands to place it aboard, as "it came with the mail and must go on with it." I was then tumbled into the car, my head downwards again, as I seemed to be destined to escape on my head; a sign probably, of the opinion of American people respecting such bold adventurers as myself; that our heads should be held downwards, whenever we attempt to benefit ourselves. Not the only instance of this propensity, on the part of the American people, towards the colored race. We had not proceeded far, however, before more baggage was placed in the car, at a stopping place, and I was again turned to my proper position. No farther difficulty occurred until my arrival at Philadelphia. I reached this place at three o'clock in the morning, and remained in the depot until six o'clock, A. M., at which time, a waggon drove up, and a person inquired for a box directed to such a place, "right side up." I was soon placed on this waggon, and carried to the house of my friend's correspondent, where quite a number of persons were waiting to receive me. They appeared to be some afraid to open the box at first, but at length one of them rapped upon it, and with a trembling voice, asked, "Is all right within?" to which I replied, "All right." The joy of these friends was excessive, and like the ancient Jews, who repaired to the rebuilding of Jerusalem, each one seized hold of some tool, and commenced opening my grave. At length the cover was removed, and I arose, and shook myself from the lethargy into which I had fallen; but exhausted nature proved too much for my frame, and I swooned away.

After my recovery from this fainting fit, the first impulse of my soul, as I looked around, and beheld my friends, and was told that I was safe, was to break out in a song of deliverance, and praise to the most high God, whose arm had been so signally manifest in my escape. Great God, was I a freeman! Had I indeed succeeded in effecting my escape from the human wolves of Slavery? O what extastic joy thrilled through every nerve and fibre of my system! My labor was accomplished, my warfare was ended, and I stood erect before my equal fellow men;[10] no longer a crouching slave, forever at the look and nod of a whimsical and tyrannical slave-owner. Long had seemed my journey, and terribly hazardous had been my attempt to gain my birth-right; but it all seemed a comparatively light price to pay for the precious boon of Liberty. O ye, who know not the value of this "pearl of great price," by having been all your life shut out from its life-giving presence; learn of how much importance its possession is regarded, by the panting fugitive, as he traces his way through the labyrinths of snares, placed between him and the object of his fond desires! Sympathize with the three millions of crushed and mangled ones who this day pine in cruel bondage, and arouse yourself to action in their behalf! This you will do, if you are not traitors to your God and to humanity. Aid not in placing in high offices, baby-stealers and women-whippers; and if these wicked men, all covered with the clotted gore of their mangled victims, come among you, scorn the idea of bowing in homage to them, whatever may be the character of their claims to your regard. No matter, if they are called presidents of your nation, still utterly refuse to honor them; which you will most certainly do, if you are true to the Slave!

After remaining a short time in Philadelphia, it was thought expedient that I should proceed to Massachusetts, and accordingly funds sufficient to carry me there, were raised by some anti-slavery friends, and I proceeded to Boston. After remaining a short time in that city, I concluded to go to New Bedford, in which place I remained a few weeks, under the care of Mr. Joseph Rickerston of that place, who treated me very kindly. At length hearing of a large anti-slavery meeting to be held in Boston, I left New Bedford, and found myself again in that city, so famous for its devotion to liberty in the days of the American revolution; and here, in the presence of several thousand people, did I first relate in public, the story of my sufferings, since which time I have repeated my simple tale in different parts of Massachusetts, and in the State of Maine.

I now stand before you as a free man, but since my arrival among you, I have been informed that your laws require that I should still be held as a slave; and that if my master should espy me in any nook or corner of the free states, according to the constitution of the United States, he could secure me and carry me back into Slavery; so that I am confident I am not safe, even here, if what I have heard concerning your laws is true. I cannot imagine why you should uphold such strange laws. I have been told that every time a man goes to the polls and votes, he virtually swears to sustain them, frightful as they are. It seems to me to be a hard case, for a man to endure what I have endured in effecting my escape, and then to be continually exposed to be seized by my master, and carried back into that horrid pit from which I have escaped. I have been told, however, that the people here would not allow me to be thus returned, that they would break their own laws in my behalf, which seems quite curious to me;

for why should you make laws, and swear to uphold them, and then break them? I do not understand much about laws, to be sure, as the law of my master is the one I have been subject to all my life, but some how, it looks a little singular to me, that wise people should be obliged to break their own laws, or else do a very wicked act. I have been told that there are twice as many voters at the North as there are at the South, and much more wealth, as well as other things of importance, which makes me study much, why the Northern people live under such laws. If I was one of them, and had any influence among them, it appears to me, I should advocate the overthrow of such laws, and the establishment of better ones in their room. Many people tell me besides, that if the slaves should rise up, and do as they did in Nat Turner's time, endeavor to fight their way to freedom, that the Northern people are pledged to shoot them down, and keep them in subjection to their masters. Now I cannot understand this, for almost all the people tell me, that they "are opposed to Slavery," and yet they swear to prevent the slaves from obtaining their liberty! If these things could be made clear to my mind, I should be glad; but a fog hangs over my eyes at present in reference to this matter.

I now wish to introduce to your hearing, a friend of mine, who will tell you more about these things than I can, until I have had more time to examine this curious subject. What he shall have to say to you, may not be as interesting as the account of my sufferings, but if you really wish to help my brethren in bondage, you will not be unwilling to hear what he may say to you, in reference to the way to abolish slavery, as you cannot be opposed to my sufferings, unless you are willing to exert yourselves for the overthrow of the cruel system which caused them.

CURE FOR THE EVIL OF SLAVERY

Dear Friends,—You have listened with eager ears, and with tearful eyes, to the recital of Mr. Brown. He has alluded to the laws which many of you uphold, when you go to the polls and vote, but he has not informed you of your duty at the present crisis. What I have to say at this time, will be mainly directed to the remedy for this terrible evil, so strikingly portrayed in his eventful life. As one of those who desire the abolition of Slavery, it is my earnest desire to be made acquainted with a true and proper remedy for this dreadful disease. I apprehend that no moral evil exists, for the cure of which there cannot be found some specific, the application of which, will effectually eradicate the disorder. I am not a politician, and cannot write as politicians do. Still I may be pardoned for entering a little into their sphere of action, for the purpose of plucking some choice fruit from the overhanging boughs of that fruitful arena. I am not afraid of politics, for I do not regard them as too sacred, or as too profane, for me to handle. I believe that the people of this country are not ready for a truly Christian government; therefore, although I cannot unite myself with any other, yet I should be rejoiced, at beholding the faintest resemblance to such an one, in opposition to our present pro-slavery government.

I would like to see all men perfect Christians, but as I do not expect to witness this sight very soon, I am gratified at their becoming anti-slavery, or even temperance men. Any advance from the old corruptions of the past, is hailed with delight by me.

The point I would now urge upon your attention is, the immediate formation of a new government at the North, at all events, and at all hazards! I do not say, "Down with this Union" merely, but I do say, up with an Anti-Slavery government, in the free States. Our object should be the establishment of a form of government, directly in opposition to the one we at present live under. The stars and stripes of our country's flag, should be trodden into the dust, and a white banner, with the words, "Emancipation to the Slaves" inscribed upon it, should be unfurled to the breeze, in the room of the old emblem of despotic servitude. Too long have we been dilatory upon this point; but the period I believe has now arrived, for us to strike for freedom, in earnest. Let us see first, what we have to accomplish; and then the means whereby we can bring about the desired end; our capabilities for such a work; and the reasons why we should adopt this plan; and what will be the consequences of such a course of action. First. What have we to accomplish? A great and an important end truly, which is nothing less, than the establishment of a new government, right in the midst of our present pro-slavery one.

A government, is a system of authority sustained by either the rulers, or the ruled, or by both conjointly. If it depends on the will of the rulers, then they can change it at pleasure; but if the people are connected with it, their consent must be gained, before its character can be altered. If, as is the case with our government, it is the people who "ordain and establish" laws, then it lies with them to change those laws, and to remodel that government. Let this fact be distinctly understood; for the majority of the people of this land, seem to labor under the delusion, that our government is sustained by some other power than their own; and are very much in the situation of those heathen nations, condemned by one of the ancient prophets, who manufactured their deities, and then fell down and worshipped the work of their own hands. The people make laws for their own guidance, and then offer as an excuse for their bad conduct, that the laws require them to do so! The government appears to be yet surrounded with a halo of glory, as it was in the days of kingly authority, when "the powers that be" were supposed to have been approvingly "ordained of God," and men fear to touch the sacred structure of their own erecting, as if God's throne would be endangered thereby. This is not the only manifestation of self-esteem connected with their movements.

The people also fancy, that what their fathers created is divine, when their fathers have departed, and left them to do as they elect, without any obligation resting upon them to follow in their steps; but so great is the self-esteem of the people, as manifested in their pride of ancestry, that they seem to suppose, that God would cast them off forever, if they should cease to be children, and become men, casting from them, the doctrines and political creeds of their fathers; and yet they boast of their spirit of progress! They fear to act for themselves, lest they should mar the reputation of their ancestors, and be deprived of their feeling of self-adulation, in consequence of the perfection of their worthy sires. But we must humble our pride, and cease worshipping, either our own, or our father's handiwork,—in reference to the laws, of which we are speaking. What we want is, a very simple thing. Our fathers proclaimed themselves free and independent of the British government, and proceeded to establish a new one, in its room. They threw off the British yoke! We can do the same, in reference to the United States government! We can put forth our "declaration of independence," and issue our manifesto of grievances; and as our fathers did, can pledge to one another, "our lives, our property and our sacred honor," in promoting the accomplishment of this end. We can immediately organize a new government, independent of the present one under which we live. We may be deemed traitors for so doing; but were not Samuel Adams and John Hancock traitors? and did not our forefathers inscribe on their banners, "resistance to tyrants is obedience to God?" Are we more faint-hearted than they were? Are not our and the slave's grievances more unendurable than were their wrongs? A new government is what we want; and the sound should go forth from all these free hills, echoing across the plains of the far distant West, that New England and the whole North, are ready to do battle with the myrmidons of the slave power, not with the sword of steel, but with the spirit of patient submission to robbery and death, in defence of our principles. We are not obliged to muster our squadrons in "hot haste," to the "sound of the cannon's deafening roar," nor to arm ourselves for physical combat; for there is more power in suffering death, for truth's sake, than in fighting with swords of steel, and with cannon balls. A new government we must have; and now let us consider, Secondly, how we shall bring this end about, and some reasons why we should adopt this course.

Step by step, do we progress in all improvements designed for man's well being. At first the people in a semi-barbarous state, are satisfied with a rude code of laws, similar to that given by a military commander, to the rough bandits under his direction; but as science unfolds its truthful wings, and spreads over the minds of the race, a mantle of wisdom, which covers their rude imperfections, and shuts out from the eye of man, their inelegant barbarities, a regard for the good opinion of others more civilized than they, induces such a people to demand the overthrow of their savage code, which they have become ashamed of acknowledging. The ancient Jews were supposed to stand in need of laws of this character; which hung over their heads, threatening the most severe punishments for the commission of, sometimes, very light crimes; as Sinai's burning mountain flashed its fierce lightnings in their awe-stricken faces, and sent forth its terrible thunders, sounding in their superstitious ears, like the voice of Deity. This people had just emerged from the depths of Egyptian slavery, and might have stood in need of such severe and terrible laws, so Draconic in their nature; but the refined inhabitants of polished Greece and Rome, needed not such barbarous enactments. The advancing spirit of civilization had swept along in its effacing train, all the necessity for such brutal ferocity, by destroying the ferocious character of the people; as it opened to them more refined sources of enjoyment, in the erection of works of art, and in mental cultivation. The muses too, had purified and rendered delicate their tastes, so that outward barbarity seemed no longer attractive; although their ancestors had indulged in such scenes with great gusto. Our Druidical, Saxon and Norman ancestry, might have needed as cruel laws as those we now live under. At least such laws would have been more appropriate to their semi-barbarous condition, than they are to our improved state; but surely, we of the nineteenth century, having outlived the errors of the past, and having reached a point, from which we can cast our eyes far back into the distant past, and behold with utter astonishment, the absurd practices of our cruel and ignorant ancestors; are not obliged, out of regard for the memory of those not so far removed from us, in point of time, as those whose memories we do not hesitate to execrate, to retain as objectionable laws as ever disgraced the statute book of England, in the days of the bloody Jeffreys, or when the unalterable "Star chamber" decisions, were the law of the land. For a country to make its boast of civilization, and to call itself a refined nation, while it tenaciously grasps the worst errors of its ancestors, and plunges into a fit of madness, at the least allusion to an alteration of its cannibal laws, seems somewhat astonishing. It makes one think of a man, who should propose joining a church, and when asked to give up dram-drinking and gambling, should break forth in a torrent of abuse, against those who made the proposition to him; for those practices are no more contrary to the sweet spirit of heavenly religion, than is slaveholding in opposition to true civilization, and perfect refinement. It is a remnant of that spirit of barbarity, which formerly induced men to fight for conquest and territory, in the palmiest days of the ancient Eastern empires, when the fields of the earth, fair mother of our existence, were made fertile by the rich streams of blood, flowing from the mangled corpses, strewn upon its surface, by the fiendish barbarity of a Sennacherib, a Cyrus, a Xerxes, and an Alexander.

An alteration of our present laws is demanded; but who will agitate this subject, where it must be agitated, in order to accomplish the end so ardently desired? It is well known, that a simple majority of votes in Congress, can never affect the alteration proposed,—that three fourths of the States of this Union must be penetrated with the spirit of repentance, in reference to slavery, and bring forth the legitimate fruit thereof, by consenting to this alteration, before it can be accomplished; and who will go to the South, that "valley of the shadow of death," in regard to all subjects having reference to man's improvement, and urge this course upon its darkened inhabitants? But this step must be taken, before the Constitution can be altered, or its meaning rendered unequivocal, so as not to be misunderstood by the authorities of this nation; for it is not to be expected that the South will ever repent of their own accord, and change the laws of the Union, because we demand it, unless the alternative is presented them, of such change, or disunion on our part.

But the time expended in converting the people of the North to a willingness to alter the Constitution, would amply suffice to persuade them to organize a new government; for the Northern people are as ready to go for a dissolution of the Union, as they are for an alteration of the Constitution; for much advance has already been made in indoctrinating them in reference to the former idea, and thousands and tens of thousands are probably converts to this doctrine, while but little or nothing has been said in reference to the latter alternative. No party has yet proposed this step; but a large and increasing one, embodying a great portion of the talent of the nation, is now earnestly engaged in advocating the former. Which would be the easiest of accomplishment then, the conversion of the North to disunion principles, or to a willingness to alter the Constitution? Every one at all versed in political affairs, must be aware, that an alteration of the Constitution, without the consent of the South, would be a virtual dissolution of the Union, even if such a step were possible; so that converting the Northern people to the doctrine of an alteration of the Constitution, would be, in fact, only another phase of conversion to disunion; for, of course, the South will never consent to such an alteration, only as an alternative, in opposition to dissolution. To be sure, if the Northern people would act as a body, and boldly say to the South, "give us an alteration of the 'three-fifths representation' clause of the Constitution; a change of that in reference to 'domestic insurrection;' and an entire destruction of the one requiring 'persons held to service, under the laws of a state,' to be given up to 'those to whom such service or labor may be due,' or we will break away from your polluting embrace;" there would probably be no need of our ever dissolving the Union, if the South believed the North was speaking truly; for, a petted and indulged child, rendered effeminate by parental fondness and neglect of all discipline, would be in no more danger of leaving forever its parent's abode, without a farthing in its pocket, or the ability to walk a single step alone, because of its parents' refusal to gratify its whims any longer; than would the "spoiled child" of the South, who has been fed on the richest viands our Northern pantry could supply, and drank of the costliest wines our free cellars could furnish, be in danger of leaving its well-supplied table of Northern spreading, and spring from the soft lap of Northern indulgence, to go forth to its own poverty-stricken lands, obliged to earn its coarse bread and clear water, by the hard toil of its own delicate hands.

But will the Northern people ever be ready to say this to the South? Not until years of patient toil in cultivating the pro-slavery soil of their hearts, have been expended by those whose office it seems to be to labor for the slaves' release; and even then, it is questionable whether, after having been supported by the North so long, and so patiently, the South would believe all our affirmations; and we after all might be obliged to withdraw from her. But if the plan we propose, should be adopted, it would save all this uncertainty, for the South would then know we meant what we said, and would be frightened at our movements; as a woman is filled with dismay, when her only protector, talks of leaving her and her helpless babes, to the cold charities of an unfeeling world.

It is certain the South never would consent to an alteration of the Constitution, unless she was driven to it by the North, which object has not yet been proposed by any Northern party; and before any great progress could be made in the reception of such a doctrine, a little knot of patriots, armed with the invincible resolution of him, whose narrative has been presented to you, or with that of our revolutionary fathers; could have erected the standard of revolt, and have formed the basis of a new and powerful government. It is not a reform in our government that we need, but a revolution—an overthrow of the present one, and the establishment of a new one. Supposing a few individuals should be hung as traitors, would not that create a sympathy for us among the governments of the old world? and would not the universal voice of all civilized nations cry out against our immolation? Let but as many individuals unite, as signed the famous manifesto of our fathers, and armed with their Spartan spirit, pledge our lives and fortunes to the accomplishment of this end! Let our declaration of independence be sent forth to all the world, and our grievances be stated in the hearing of mankind! Let a new Continental Congress meet, at some favorable point, draft a new Constitution, and all who drink of the spirit of liberty, which flowed into the hearts of our fathers, be requested to annex their names to the document! Let it go forth to the whole land as our Constitution! Let immediate measures be taken for an active and efficient agitation of the whole subject; our orators to go forth, and in the streets and lanes of our cities and villages, proclaim the object we have in view; or, if a more silent way of proceeding shall be deemed the most expedient, let committees visit every house and shop in our land, and see who will gird on this armor, and resolve to perish in an attempt to rescue the bleeding slave, from the hands of his cruel master, by refusing all support to this government, even to the deprivation of the necessaries of life.

And now comes the period of our proposed bloodless revolution, which will try men's souls. Let us do as our fathers did, and refuse to pay taxes to the general government. "Millions for defence, but not one cent for tribute," cried our ancestors, in order to save their descendants from the oppressive spirit of England's grasping avarice. They at first were ridiculed, and it is stated that when John Warren, one of the aristocracy of Boston, made an inflammatory speech, at a rebel meeting, that he was denounced by the leading citizens of this place, and a copy of a letter is still preserved, written by some of them in reference to the transaction, in which they state, that "one Dr. Warren, had indeed made a rebellious speech, but he was applauded only by a few rowdies." Shall not we be as willing to sacrifice our property and lives, as were our ancestors? Did not John Hancock hand the keys of his stores and dwelling to the authorities of the city, saying to them, "this is all of my property, but if the good of Boston requires its destruction, I freely yield it to you?" To pay taxes is to support the government, under which we live, for without this support it could not exist. These taxes are not paid of course directly, but still we eat, drink, and wear those things, on which a duty is paid, which gives the general government all its power. For instance. The Mexican War has left a large debt resting on our shoulders. The only way in which it will be paid probably is, by an increased tariff on particular articles of consumption. Now if an entire cessation of such consumption should take place, would not the government be left destitute of the means to pay this debt? Who pays the salaries of the officers of this government, but the consumer of the articles taxed by it? If the consumption of all such articles can be prevented, would not our government be obliged to cease operations, for want of oil to grease its machinery with? It moves only as money is furnished it.

Our navy and army, the protectors of the South, can only be supported by large sums of money, derived from the revenue of the nation, which revenue we help to create by our consumption of these things. If sugar pays a large duty, or tea and coffee, or silks and satins, broadcloths and cassimeres, by refusing to use those articles, and inducing others to do the same, would not the revenue of the nation be affected? and when the actual tax-gatherer in the shape of the merchant, holds out his seductive wares for our purchase, could we not exhibit to him our pledge to "totally abstain" from the use of such articles; as the temperance man shows his ticket, as a reason why he should not partake of the intoxicating cup?

Another step could also be taken. A president could be chosen by us, and other necessary officers, and we could go on with our government, just as if no other existed, "beating for recruits" all the while, and offering no physical resistance to those who molest us. Have we not a right so to do? "Children of the glorious dead! Who for freedom fought and bled," have you become bond slaves to a power fully as oppressive of you, as that of Britain's tyrannical king, against whom your ancestors lifted their stout arms in rebellion, and unfurled their banner of revolt, on which was gloriously inscribed, "victory or death?" Have you forever lost all that portion of your ancestral fire, which armed three millions of poor and feeble men to engage in deadly combat with the richest and most powerful nation in Christendom? Ah, has God forsaken you so entirely, that no pulse of gladness beats in your frame, as you listen to the stirring notes of the wild, clarion sound of freedom, coming over these hills, and echoing from the far-distant prairies of the wide West? Oh is there not, friends, any deep fountain of sorrow gushing up from the inmost depths of your secret souls, for the sufferings and woes of the three millions of your Southern brethren? Ah, is there not any remnant of the spark of divinity which our Father in heaven has placed in every human heart, left to warm up your frigid souls? Say, breathes there not a particle of indignant life in your moral nature, as you listen to the mad agonies of shrieking mothers, the victims of remorseless tyrants who now stand defacing God's image and stamping in the dust the lineaments of their Creator? Oh, is there none of manhood left in you, that the shrieks of trampled upon and bleeding innocence, should not move you to contend with Slavery's cruel power? But is not your own safety a reason why you should cease to doff your beavers to the South, and should refuse to pay homage to her any longer? Listen a moment while I exhibit to you some more personal and selfish arguments. At the last election, the Southern States were allowed one electoral vote for every 7,500 voters, while at the North, it took 12,000 voters to entitle us to one elector. The number of electors, of which we were thus deprived, was about 100, which was the same as excluding from the privilege of the elective franchise, 750,000 voters, about the number in all New England and Pennsylvania! Now are not these persons taxed equally with those who have the privilege of voting? Do not all the citizens of the North pay taxes? Yes, and much more than their true proportion, for by far the greater portion of duty-paying goods, are consumed at the North. Then, is not the principle which our fathers died to oppose, fully carried out by our government, taxation without representation? and yet we tamely submit to this plucking our substance from us, by the fierce beak of our country's eagle; while our fathers would not so much as listen to the slight growling of the English lion, as he shook his shaggy mane in their faces, and touched them with but the extremities of his bloody paw! Robbery, if committed by a bird of prey, the American eagle, is to be patiently submitted to, and indeed we call it but the tickling of an affectionate friend or child; but let the valiant lion of Old England take the value of a pin's point, or a few old pine trees and worthless rocks from us, and how the welkin rings with the sound of our abhorrence of such depredations. We are like the slaveholder, spoken of in our friend's narrative, who told the slaves it was a crime to steal from him, but none to rob his neighbors, because he reaped the benefits of the theft. So with us. We are rewarded for our submission to this robbery, by the paltry trade of the South, and as long as a few of us can make more money than we lose otherwise by our connection with the South, we care not for our principles, although every fourth of July we laud our fathers for fighting in behalf of them; or for the losses of the mass of the people. Taxation without representation! This practice deluged the fields of our country, with our ancestor's and Briton's son's blood; and caused our prosperity, as a nation, to be stricken to the ground, and we magnify our fathers for their boldness, in reference to it; yet we cherish the same principle, and press it to our bosoms as a part of our religion!

Great Britain tried our fathers, accused of crime, away from their homes, across the waters of the ocean, and we call it a great oppression; but let one of our sons be guilty of an act in violation of Southern law, or be even suspected of it, and there is no law by which he can be tried. All law is trampled under foot, and he is doomed to waste away his life, in a gloomy prison, or to be whipped almost to death. Which is the worst, being tried across the sea, by an impartial court, or being strung up by Lynch law between the heavens and the earth, and left dangling on the limb of a tree, or else doomed to wear out a miserable existence in some foul dungeon?

But to make the case still more parallel. Great Britain, our fathers complained, quartered soldiers upon them in times of peace, who eat out their substance and corrupted the people. For what other earthly purpose is the army of the United States continued in existence, but to watch the bidding of the monster Slavery, and be ready to fly at a moment's warning to her assistance, in case the least attempt should be made by their victims to regain their freedom? That this is a true statement, may be seen from the fact, that all our wars for the last thirty-five years, have been waged in behalf of Slavery, and even our last war with Great Britain, is attributed by many persons to the demands of the slave power. It is certain, that no war will ever be allowed by the South, except in behalf of Slavery, for it would be detrimental to their interests; and it is well known that she rules over the destinies of this country, and guides its affairs of state, as effectually as Alexander or Napoleon ruled the countries they had conquered. Slavery rules this nation, did we say? It can hardly be called ruling, for we are so submissive to the faintest manifestation of her will, that she has but to glance her glowing eye towards our craven souls, and we will prostrate our abject forms lowly on the ground, with our faces hid in the dust, which we are truly unworthy to touch; as submissively and reverentially, as the devout Mussulman kisses the ground when the hour of prayer arrives, crying, "God is great." Our God is emphatically Slavery. To him we address our early matins, and in his ear are uttered our evening orisons. More devoutly do we render homage to our god, Slavery, than the most pious of us adore the God of heaven, which proves that we are a very religious people, worshipping, not crocodiles, leeks and onions, snakes, and images of wood and stone, but a god, whose service is infinitely more disgusting than that of any heathen idol, but one who pays us well, for our obeisance, as we imagine.

In this matter of a standing army, we go beyond our fathers in suffering oppression. They were not obliged to fight for England, when the object of the war was to enslave themselves; but it is well known that the great object the South has in view, in all her wars, is the aggrandizement of herself and the subjection of the North to her complete dictation; and we are called upon to engage in these wars, and after they are fought, we are compelled to foot the heavy bills.

But when our fathers were oppressed, they could plead in their own behalf. If they placed their feet on England's shores, no harm could befal them, as long as they were guilty of no crime. They could defend their own cause; and the thunders of a Burke's eloquence, shook the walls of Parliament to their foundation, and made the tyrants of England tremble and quake with fear, as he poured forth the fervor of his vehement eloquence in strong condemnation of the oppression of the colonies. A William Pitt too, could frighten the British minister from his unhallowed security, amid the multitude of fawning sycophants surrounding him, in the height of his political power, by the thunders of his voice, uttered in faithful rebuke of the war measures of the government. This noble Earl, was allowed to plead in behalf of American freedom, until his earnest spirit was claimed by the grim messenger death, as he arose in his place in the House of Lords, to speak in our behalf. But suffer what we may, is there any redress for us at the hands of our government? Our property may be injured by spoliations on our commerce, such as imprisoning our seamen, as well as by the crime of seizing our free citizens and depriving them of their liberty; and can we obtain the least redress? O the ignominy of our puerile connection with the South!

It is well known that under the system of Slavery, the three great blessings of republicanism are denied to a large portion of our citizens. These are, freedom of the press, of speech and of locomotion. And will we allow ourselves to be deprived of what even Europe's despotic kings have been bestowing upon their subjects? Are we more base and abject in our submission to the South, than are the oppressed millions of the old world, in their subjection to their kingly oppressors? O what falsifiers of our own professions, and truants to our own dearly prized principles, we are! Can an abolitionist travel unexposed at the South? I have had some little experience in the matter, and know that such is not the case. Men have pursued me with relentless hate, and implements of death have been brought into requisition against me, for no crime, only for exposing Slavery, in its own dominions. Can we send to any part of the South those newspapers we may wish to send there? While at the South, I was advised by a friend to conceal a paper I had received, because of its being opposed to Slavery; and it is in only particular portions of that ill-fated country, that anti-slavery publications, can be introduced. It is not many years, since a man was publicly whipped, for having an anti-slavery newspaper wrapped around a bible, which he was offering for sale. As to liberty of speech, not half the freedom is allowed the opponents of Slavery on the floors of Congress, that the British Parliament allowed the opposers of the American War. In Boston, on the day which ushered the famous stamp act into existence, the bells were tolled, and a funeral procession passed through the streets, bearing a coffin, on which the word Liberty was inscribed. "During the movement of the procession, minute guns were fired, and an oration was pronounced in favor of the deceased. Similar expressions of grief and indignation occurred in many parts of the land;" but, friends, no funeral procession passed through our streets when Liberty died the second time—no muffled bells sounded their melancholy peals in the ears of a mourning people; no liberty-loving orator was found to pronounce a requiem for the departed goddess; and yet she was slain—and slain too, not by foreign hands, nor by the natural allies of human oppressors, but, shall I tell the sad and dismal tale? by those, who twenty-five years before, had shrouded their faces in mantles of mourning, and rent the air with their expressions of grief, at the destruction of one of liberty's little fingers, by the passage of the stamp act; but when Liberty lay a full length corpse, on the floors of that Congress, which sold her to the South, as Judas betrayed the Son of God, and for almost as small a boon, viz.: "the carrying trade" of the South; not only were there no lamentations made over her complete departure, but she was taken by night and buried hastily; while "Not a drum was heard nor a funeral note," as her corse was deposited without a "winding sheet," or even "a soldier's cloak" to wrap around her bleeding form. Clandestinely was she hurried out of the sight of the men who murdered her; and instead of songs of sorrow, being heard throughout the land, praise ascended from its every corner, and honors were heaped on the heads of her murderers.

But Liberty as truly died then, as if loud lamentations had been made in her behalf, and the descendants of those very men, who in 1765 followed the coffin of liberty to its place of deposit, because no business was deemed lawful unless the records of it were made on stamped paper; the descendants of these very mourners of liberty, now, do what is infinitely worse than to use the stamped paper of a British king; they swear to support that sacrifice of Liberty upon the altar of Southern slavery, whenever they are admitted to any offices of trust and renown. Is not this oppressive, when we may not administer justice to our fellow men, or exercise the most common authority, without renewing the thrust at the departed spirit of liberty, as our fathers actually slew her fair form?

O Liberty! didst thou draw thy keen sword

For those, whom av'rice sought to rob, and slay,

And sent its minions far, to seek its prey,

That glittering gold might its coffers fill;

While they their foes should crush, and seek to kill,

That England's lords, their gold could steal, and hoard?

Goddess celestial, and divine, and pure,

Wert thou, the champion brave, the soldier true,

Who fought with youthful vigor, with the few,

Of Columbia's sons, who stood, a sturdy band,

And bade their country's foes to leave their land,

While they, to thee didst vow allegiance sure?

Insulted nymph! thy fair form shone so bright,

That kings, as thee they saw, could not reject

That face, alive with claims to their respect;

E'en they, besotted with the lust of power,

Could not refuse to yield to thee thy dower,

But ceased at thy command, their foes to fight.

But ah! the men who thee so loud did call,

The souls, whom thou hadst saved from bondage dread,

O fearful tale! themselves on thee did tread;

And thy fair robe was pierced with traitorous thrusts.

As Caesar groaning fell and kissed the dust,

When ingrate Brutus' blows on him did fall.

On the 5th of March, 1775, the Boston massacre occurred—the fearful tragedy of State Street! All Boston was aroused, murders dreadful had been committed by the British troops, and it was a difficult task to allay the excitement occasioned thereby. What was the amount of this terrible massacre? Why, three Boston citizens had been shot in the heat of an affray with the British soldiery! What horror seemed to seize upon the hearts of the people! Why, "our brothers are being shot down in the face of open day, and our turn may come next." Terrible was the indignation of our fathers! And yet we, their descendants, calmly allow the South to slay our citizens at their leisure. The blood of a murdered Lovejoy, still cries out from the ground for vengeance! A Baltimore prison, still contains the impress of a departed spirit's feet, which left an impression on its gloomy pavement, as he fled from an earthly prison-house to the mansions of the blest. A C. C. Torrey still calls for redress for his wrongs at the hands of Southern tyrants. The jail of our own capital if it could speak, would tell of him who pined away within its noisome walls, as he lay in that republican enclosure, a victim to Southern tyranny. Yes, Dr. Crandall's blood has not yet been atoned for, by the wicked South. Here are, at least three victims who have been slain, at the cruel dictation of Slavery's dreadful power. But time would fail me, to tell of a Van Zandt, of a Fairbanks, and of numerous others, whose lives have been forfeited to the South. And yet we submit to her dictation. Our own citizens slain, imprisoned, and cruelly beaten, but yet we have no heart to break away from this degrading alliance with our Southern man-stealing brethren.

But, I must bring this expostulation to a close, and proceed to show the consequences of this event, the formation of a new government. Of these it may be said; they could not be more disastrous to the North than Slavery has been; for like the "horse-leech's two daughters," she continually cries "give, give," and never seems to have enough. Hardly through with the digestion of the tremendous morsel just administered to her gormandizing appetite, she commences to lick her lips, and daintily ask for a dessert, with which to finish the full meal which she has already made of California and New Mexico, and as her mother deems it her duty, never to deny any of her darling daughter's reasonable requests, probably the Island of Cuba, will soon be placed at her side, for her to nibble upon at leisure.

Many persons deprecate our plan, for fear of a civil war; and terrific ideas of rivers of blood rolling across our fields, and piles of bones heaped on our shores, startle them in their slumbers, as the rustling of a leaf fills the slaveholder's heart with fear. In the first place, how very absurd is this idea of a civil war being the result of disunion. Can any one seriously urge it, as an objection to this movement? Look at the vast extent of territory open to the incursions of an enemy, if the North should withdraw from the South. There are the Islands of the West Indies, filled with emancipated slaves, ready, some of them to join in an effort to redeem the Southern slaves from bondage. Then there is the long line of sea-board, entirely unprotected, which even in the last war was devastated in part by the British army, and the capital of our country reduced to ashes. On the Northern frontier, runs that talismanic line, over which a slave has but to place his foot, and glorious liberty becomes his possession. Here stand, twelve millions of freemen, ready to fight in behalf of the panting fugitive, while nearly 20,000 sturdy hearts beat quick to the sound of the trumpet of freedom, and are ready to leave their homes in Canada, to assist their brethren. Then, there is ill-treated and insulted Mexico, burning under a sense of the wrongs inflicted upon her, and watching an opportunity to redress those wrongs. Last of all, are the numerous Indian tribes, smarting under a deep sense of the wrongs they have received at our hands. Now will any sensible person assert that five millions of Southerners, allowing all her white population to be in favor of Slavery, with an intestine foe, ready to spring upon her, as soon as the last chance of freedom presents itself, will be in danger of fighting twelve millions of free Northerners, who can call to their aid all these, and numerous other allies? Why, the idea is preposterous, and none but an insane man, can seriously entertain it. Who would fight the North, if war should be declared? At the first sound of the trumpet of war, every slave would be instantly free; for never could the Southerners leave their homes exposed to the fury of an insurgent population, as they would be obliged to, if an army should be organized to fight the North.

But who are those persons who cry out "civil war, and bloodshed?" Are they not mostly those who believe the revolutionary war to have been right? If Slavery is wrong, to be consistent, they ought to hail any movement which will hasten an insurrection among the Slaves. What is a civil war of a few years' continuance, in comparison to the seven years' war we waged with Great Britain? Then our resources were limited, our treasury light, and we were only three millions strong. But now, we abound in resources, have become plethoric on account of our riches, and are twelve millions strong, while our enemy is less than half that number. We coped with twenty millions of British subjects, when we numbered but three millions, can we not now with twelve millions cope with five? Then has our glory departed indeed, and we are the veriest slaves in existence. But would our trade be endangered? Ah, that is the question. Said a person to me not long since, "I acknowledge there would be benefits in a dissolution of the Union, but there are also disadvantages." And what are they? we inquired. "Why, our trade would be injured." Let it perish then! Every mother's son of us, had better pack up and on board our numerous vessels go on a begging expedition to England or France, or we had better "tie millstones about our necks, and drown ourselves in the depths of the sea;" or, we had better lay down in the streets and perish with hunger, than to allow Slavery to continue its existence.

The moment it is granted that a dissolution of the Union would abolish Slavery quicker than any other course, then I think our point is gained, and there is no necessity of proving that we shall not lose the sale of a few hats and boots, or slave whips. It seems almost an insult to the character of the Northern people to answer such an argument as this, and yet I fear that it is the "strong reason" why this question meets with so much opposition.

If slavery is abolished, no one can deny that our trade, so important to Northern men, and for which they are ready to barter the welfare of three millions of human beings, would be materially increased; but for one I care not, whether this will be the case or not. I cannot, I will not argue this question. It is a sin against the Holy Ghost, to dream of balancing the matter in this way. Northern men, you are too much actuated by this spirit of Avarice! You must be converted from this accursed love for gold; for it will sink you into the lowest degradation of a life afar from Deity. You cannot be the friends of God, while it reigns in your hearts! You must arise, and cast it from you! You must be converted from your selfishness, and then you will have no objections to offer against a dissolution of the Union! If your eyes can only be anointed with the eye-salve of humanity, and be washed in the waters of benevolence, you will see the folly of all your objections, and will be ready to sink all your ships with their rich cargoes, into the depths of the sea, and to burn your well-filled stores, rather than to cause Slavery to continue another day! O, men of the North, can ye not be aroused to action in the slave's behalf? Shall the purple streams of the slave's blood, flow ceaselessly and rapidly o'er our land, gushing forth from every hill-side of the South, and coloring all the fair fields of Southern industry, on account of your sustaining power? O that I could utter some word in your ear, which would quicken your dormant sensibilities and arouse you to action in the slave's cause! Shall I tell you of God, of heaven, and of hell? There is a God, and as he descends from his abode among the stars, and essays to find an entrance into your soul, by which he may make you "a joint heir with Christ to an inheritance, incorruptible and undefiled and which fadeth not away," depend upon it, that he will be frustrated in his benevolent purpose, if the demon of pro-slavery, lies coiled up in your heart. Whatever may be said of religion, it is true that God can never approve of any person, in league with slaveholders; for a just God is forever opposed to all forms of robbery and oppression. If God's favor then is of any value, flee, I beseech thee, to the arms of liberty, and be encircled by her protecting power; so that all approach to Slavery may be dreaded by thee, as an angel dreads the polluting touch of sin.

FOOTNOTES

[1] HUGO GROTIUS was, in the year 1620, sent from prison, confined in a small chest of drawers, by the affectionate hands of a faithful wife, but he was taken by friends on horseback and carried to the house of a friend, without undergoing much suffering or running the terrible risk which our friend ran.

[2] The reader may be disposed to doubt the truth of the above assertion, but I once asked a girl in Ky., whose mistress was a Methodist church member, if she could tell me "who Jesus Christ was?" "Yes," said she, "he is the bad man."

[3] In proof of this, I would state that during my residence at the South, a whole town was once thrown into an uproar by my entering a slave hut, about Christmas time, and talking and praying with the inmates about an hour. I was told that it would not be safe for me to remain in the town over night.

[4] While at the South, a gentleman came one day to a friend of mine, and in a very excited manner said to him, "Why, are you not afraid to have that man about you? Do you not fear that your house will be burned? I cannot sleep nights lest the slaves should rise and burn, all before them."

[5] While in Kentucky I knew of a case where a preacher punished a female slave in this way, and his wife stood by, throwing cold water into the slave's face, to keep her from fainting. In endeavoring to escape afterwards, the poor creature became faint from loss of blood, and her body was found partly devoured by the buzzards.

[6] Will not this be considered a sufficient exhibition of that charity, which pro-slavery divines exhort abolitionists to practise?

[7] Reader, do you wonder at abolitionists calling such churches the brotherhood of thieves?

[8] I would here state, that Mr. Brown is endeavoring to raise money to purchase his family. Twelve hundred dollars being the sum demanded for them. Any person wishing to assist him in this laudable purpose, can enclose donations to him, directing No. 21 Cornhill, Boston.

[9] Reader, smile not at the above idea, for if there is a God of love, we must believe that he suggests steps to those who apply to him in times of trouble, by which they can be delivered from their difficulty. I firmly believe this doctrine, and know it to be true from frequent experience.

[10] For a corroboration of this part of Mr. Brown's narrative, the reader is referred to the close of this book.

www.ingramcontent.com/pod-product-compliance
Lightning Source LLC
Chambersburg PA
CBHW021131080526
44587CB00012B/1227